A FREE
AND ORDERED
SPACE

A FREE
AND ORDERED
SPACE

The Real World of the University

A. BARTLETT GIAMATTI

⇥⇥⇥ ⇤⇤⇤

W. W. NORTON & COMPANY

New York • London

Most of the contents previously appeared, in somewhat different form and in some cases under different titles, in the *Yale Alumni Magazine*. Several of the essays previously appeared, in somewhat different form and in some cases under different titles, in *The University and the Public Interest*.

The text of this book is composed in Sabon, with display type set in Deroos Inline Initials. Composition and manufacturing by Arcata Graphics. Book design by Charlotte Staub.

First published as a Norton paperback 1990

Library of Congress Cataloging-in-Publication Data

Giamatti, A. Bartlett.
A free and ordered space: the real world of the university / A. Bartlett Giamatti.—1st ed.
p. cm.
1. Education, Higher—United States—Aims and objectives.
2. Education, Humanistic—United States. 3. Academic freedom—United States. I. Title.
LA227.3.G53 1988
378.73—dc 19   88–10013

ISBN 0-393-30671-2

W. W. Norton & Company, Inc.
500 Fifth Avenue, New York, N.Y. 10110
W. W. Norton & Company Ltd.
37 Great Russell Street, London WC1B 3NU

2 3 4 5 6 7 8 9 0

FOR
William C. Brainard

⇶ Contents ⇸

> 9 <

Preface

*T*his volume does not pretend to fill the vacuum that I will assert exists with regard to higher education's nature and purpose. Nor does it presume to contain all the answers, either to the questions I pose or to all the questions posed by others. I am neither a philosopher nor a historian of education. The essays gathered here, almost all written in the years between the late seventies and late eighties, represent one man's effort to speak up, to say from the viewpoint of one partial and imperfect university president what he thought about the nature and purpose of the American university, about the principles of an undergraduate education, and about the pressures and affiliations connecting the university to our society. Most of these essays are concerned with the need for connectedness within institutions of higher education, and between them and other institutions; with the threat to institutional independence and interdependence from Zealots of Left or Right; about the need for an educational process that constantly tests the values it holds dear, that tolerates ambiguity and diversity in the real world—in itself and elsewhere—and that strives ever for purposeful change, change rooted in the past and blossoming throughout a lifetime.

Two cautionary notes: these essays were originally addressed for the most part to Yale students. The reader will hear occasionally and will, I hope, forgive the hortatory tone of one who was for years an enthusiastic classroom teacher. The reader will also often encounter the name *Yale*. While these essays have been revised (and in several cases significantly reduced or combined) in an effort to make them less parochial, many references to Yale remain. These references are there because I wish a certain circumstantiality, a particularity, to remain and because I do not intend Yale every time the name appears. When I wrote the essays, I hoped that in *Yale* the well-meaning reader, not gripped by the place in New Haven, might also see, where appropriate, *College* or *University*. I dared to hope Yale would be emblematic in certain respects.

The other cautionary note: I use the word *civility* often. The word is important to my view of the University as a place where the most free-swinging and intense intellectual exchange takes place without any intent to damage or coerce other human beings, and as a place where the larger goal of intellectual training is a civic one—the making not only of future scholars but of good citizens. Civility has to do with decency and mutual respect and, finally, with a free and ordered common life—or civilization. Civility has nothing at all to do with gentility, any more than citizenship, in all its resonance, has to do with good breeding or polite manners. Anyone troubling to remind him-

or herself of the respective etymologies of the two words will see the difference, and whence each derives. I make this note because I learned at Yale there were those who would insist to the contrary if not reminded that words have longer histories, and have accreted more significance, than in the seizure of the moment some choose to think.

I am grateful to many who have over the years listened to or read these essays and who have helped. May I thank particularly Toni S. Giamatti and Henry W. Broude. These essays also benefited from Mary Lou Risley, who never wearied of each iteration. Mildred Marmur was staunch and skillful in guiding them to the publisher. Barry Wade has been a superb editor. I also thank the successive generations of students who not only listened but also reacted, which is, of course, the whole point to the enterprise.

INTRODUCTION

⟫ Ruminations on University Presidency ⟪

Being president of a university is no way for an adult to make a living. Which is why so few adults actually attempt to do it. It is to hold a mid-nineteenth-century ecclesiastical position on top of a late-twentieth-century corporation. But there are those lucid moments, those crystalline experiences, those Joycean epiphanies, that reveal the numinous beyond and lay bare the essence of it all. I have had those moments. They were all moments of profound and brilliant failure—but string those glistening moments of defeat into a strand and you have the pearls of an administrative career.

In the six months between being named president of Yale University in December of 1977 and taking office in July of 1978, I had ample opportunity to receive advice. I listened to many people. I learned about the corporate world. I learned that because the corporate world is interested only in quarterly results, it talks a great deal about long-range planning. It was clear to me that Yale needed some of that, too. We needed a corporate strategy; we needed a policy. I, of course, had no policies. I had a mortgage and one suit, but no policies. I cast about. I solicited data and forecasts and projections and models. I did comparative studies, longitudinal studies; I made a flowchart and convened a task force. I hired and fired management consultants. I went in search of a policy. What was it that Yale needed most, wanted most, and would most contribute to solving our deficit, enhancing our quality, and making me a Manager?

One night in early April 1978, crouched in my garage, as I was trying to memorize the Trustees' names, particularly the ones I had met, it came to me, and I wrote, right there, between the lawnmower and the snow tires, a memo. On July 1, 1978, my first day in office, I issued this memo to an absent and indifferent University. It read,

To the members of the University Community:

In order to repair what Milton called the ruin of our grand parents, I wish to announce that henceforth, as a matter of University policy, evil is abolished and paradise is restored.

I trust all of us will do whatever possible to achieve this policy objective.

.

The reaction was quite something.

Four young members of the faculty in Comparative Literature wrote an open letter to the *New York Review of Books* proving that Milton was talking not about evil in *Paradise Lost* but about irony and the patriarchal abuse of power. A junior in Yale College, spending the summer doing a leveraged buyout of a Tastee-Freez in Easthampton, wrote me a gracious letter. She recognized the pressure one was under to have a business plan, but she hoped that I would wait until she had graduated before changing things very much. An alumnus in New York, on Yale Club stationery, wondered why the hell we always had to get so far out in front.

In September, the *Yale Daily News* wrote the first editorial about my memo. Its opening sentences were these:

> Giamatti's administration is off to a miserable start. Rather than giving us control over our lives, or at least addressing concerns of students such as the crying need for a student center so we can make friends or any of the myriad of other injustices that riddle the fabric of the quality of life here, the new administration is insensitive and repressive and the future bodes aweful.

Though one of the best-written of the *News* editorials, it was, be fair, also the first.

Since the students were back and the *Daily News* was publishing, the major media outlets now had a source for news. Student stringers went to work, and my memo achieved National Visibility. In a small article bylined "Special to The New York Times," the country's newspaper of record misspelled my name and said a Harvard professor had found a letter from Milton to his parents in the Yale Library. The *Washington Post* ran a picture of the memo in the Style section and wrote a sidebar in a box, quoting an FDA lawyer as asserting that evil had been abolished three years earlier, that the regulations had been printed in the *Federal Register,* and that nobody he knew believed evil was bad for you in any case. The *Wall Street Journal* wrote a pithy editorial pointing out that fat, liberal, effete, Marxist-oriented Eastern universities, and Stanford, too, were all in a plot to undermine the Republic, free enterprise, and greenmail as we know it today. "What we need," said the *Journal*, "is not more talk about evil, but some decent courses in risk arbitrage." George Will wrote a column citing Montesquieu, Thomas Aquinas, Locke, and Ernie Banks; William Buckley said Milton is "all very well, but it is typical of president Giamatti and his ilk to cite a secular authority on evil as if, of course, those who have passed any time down in the agora or out on the Rialto needed an authority to know the palpability of evil in all its camaraderie and liberal camouflages." In the *New Yorker*'s Talk of the Town, there was a long account about the birthday party given in a secret, nuclear-free place for Daniel Berrigan by David Dellinger; the correspondent noted in passing the nonexistence of evil in New Haven, but added that all at the party agreed that when *they* awoke that morning on Central Park West, there was certainly evil still rampant everywhere *they* could see, and their doormen had confirmed it when asked.

As you know, a university president has responsibility not only for the internal workings of the institution but also for external representation and relations as well. Of all the moments I remember—speaking to alumni, visiting foundations and corporations, mayors and governors and private individuals; going to high schools and boardrooms and newspapers and dinners and receptions—the moment I remember best is the morning I saw Congressman Phlange, from the third district of a state we will call Grace.

The Congressman's office is a series of dark paneled warrens, each leading to the other. As I enter, I see two reception desks piled high with brochures for bus tours of Arlington. On the wall is a framed poster of the last major Arts Festival held in the district—on August 17, 1937. There are two chairs, a table with copies of the *Machinists International Newsletter* and *Collier's,* and a telephone that cannot call anything. There is no ashtray.

The first receptionist is reading her high school yearbook and drinking a Diet Sprite, so I approach the other receptionist, who is less busy.

"Mr. Giamatti to see the Congressman, please," I say. She is wearing a button that says *I am a Phlangist.* She looks up and says, "He's either in the District or on the floor. They're not sure."

I sit in the corner by the phone. Suddenly the inner door opens and a middle-aged person with eyeglasses hung on a green cord around her neck and carrying an appointment book, a clipboard, a stack of letters, a cup of coffee, and a Snoopy lunch box comes up to me, says, "He'll see you now, please follow me," and takes me out the door, down the hall to the right, and through the first door we come to. We go past a word processor on an empty desk, down a short corridor filled with overflowing wastebaskets, then a sharp right, past a young man methodically shredding what looks like mail, and into the Congressman's office.

The Congressman is reading behind a huge desk, surrounded by plaques, awards, tropies, pictures, laminated scrolls, and autographed footballs. There are four easy chairs, a chocolate-colored wastebasket, an American flag, and a mother-of-pearl paperweight the size of a softball with *Republic of China* in blue letters across the base.

"Doctor, how are you. It's a pleasure. Please sit down.

Can we get you some coffee. What brings you to Washington." He has not yet looked up. "I'd like to get a picture of us together. I'll find the photographer." And suddenly he is gone, vanished out the door.

Then he is back, with a wizened photographer whose complexion reminds me of a legal pad. And a tall, slim woman, about thirty, in slacks, a blue work shirt, a denim vest, boots, her dark hair pulled back in a bun. "Doctor, this is Ms. Incomparable Worth, my legislative assistant for education. She'll sit in. Now, if you'll stand here, Doctor, we'll get a picture. I'll want several so you can write on one and I can write on one. There." A flash has gone off. The photographer leaves.

Ms. Worth speaks. "We think the NIH cuts should go through. We're not impressed with your fatuous argument that we can't change the rules halfway through the game. We believe student aid benefits only the rich and the poor; rather than stopping abuse, we'd rather do away with everything. We are for cutting out charitable deductions, for instituting the 2 percent floor, and for forbidding gifts of appreciated assets. We do not believe in a federal science facilities fund or in the nonprofit postal subsidy; we think it would be the height of fraud and abuse to fund the Humanities. We intend to uncap retirement, cap technology transfer, cut the NEA and NSF, get rid of the Library of Congress, and slash the Health Manpower Act. We want to get this country moving again."

The Congressman beams. "Doctor, let me tell you it is an honor having you here. We have a college in the district; they do a wonderful job. Education is a wonderful thing. Made the country what it is today. Look what we've got— a huge deficit, unbalanced trade, weak dollar, corruption in church and state—separated, of course. Anything I can do, tell me. Great to see you."

I went back, past the young man, shredding, past the wastebaskets, past the silent word processor, into the hall. Though I had not said a word, I had done what I came to do. I had had my picture taken, seen a staffer, met a congressman, heard all the issues touched definitively. Our system is working. The visit remains in the mind as a pearl.

There is only one other moment that stands out: a brief, but glistening, half hour, not long before I left, with a university-wide, community-based, self-selected group called the Standing Committee on Special Interests. This committee is the special-interest group that convenes to pursue a special interest if there is no preexistent special-interest group empowered to pursue that special interest. It monitors public utterances to see who might be offended, and then it takes offense if no one else has the time or inclination; it watches power structures; it petitions for redress; it rallies, gathers, assembles, queries, blockades, and even assaults sincerely in good causes. It is an extraordinarily hardworking group, never at rest, always vigilant. Recently, the Standing Committee had taken up the cause of the inequality of income distribution in North America, the preservation of all stained-glass windows at Yale, women's volleyball, structural unemployment in the Northeast, word processing terminals in the Law School, and World Hunger.

I was summoned to meet the Standing Committee. I said I would meet them in the Trustee Room, near where I had my office. They said they were not sure they could all fit in the room. I said they could send delegates; they said they did not trust each other enough to delegate any of their number. I said it was up to them. They canceled. Some clergy in town petitioned on their behalf. We agreed to meet. When they finally arrived, there were only seven of them. I asked what I could do. A long silence. "What is the issue?" I was baffled. Finally, the spokesperson said, "We are sorry to come to you like this, but we are very deeply concerned that no one in the administration is paying any attention to the most pressing problem of our time. The problem of evil and the restoration of Paradise." "But," I said, "we tried to solve that. I sent a memo on that years ago." "We weren't here years ago," said the spokesperson. "We are here now. What can we do to make it better?" We talked long into the night.

In some ways, this conversation and my parodies of all the others are variations upon that serious and splendid conversation that is any great college or university, anywhere in the country. The university today is very different from the one twenty-five years ago, or fifty or one hundred or two hundred and fifty years ago, and yet it is not different. It is still a constant conversation between young and old, between students, among faculty; between faculty and students; a conversation between past and present, a conversation the culture has with itself, on behalf of the country. The university lives through all its voices—and the conversation does not stop there, nor does our conversation with what we took away stop.

Perhaps it is the sound of all those voices, over centuries overlapping, giving and taking, that is finally the music of civilization, the sound of human beings shaping and sharing, mooring ideals to reality, making the world, for all its pain, work. The university is the place where the seeds of speech first grow and where most of us first began to find a voice. It is neither a paradise nor the worst spot we have ever been in; it is a good place that continues to want to make her children better.

Its essence is that give-and-take, that civil conversation in its innumerable forms. When that conversation, the to-and-fro of ideas, is stymied or foreclosed or frozen, when the questing for truth is told that it must cease because there is only one Truth and it is Complete, then the institution in its essence is chilled and its life threatened. Of all the threats to the institution, the most dangerous come from within. Not the least among them is the smugness that believes the institution's value is so self-evident that it no longer needs explication, its mission so manifest that it no longer requires definition and articulation.

Without constant attempts to redefine and reassert publicly their nature and purpose, universities become frozen in internal mythology, in a complacement self-perpetuation. Universities are profoundly conservative institutions, meant to transmit the past, built to remember (despite a tendency within themselves to amnesia). When they are not challenged within themselves to justify themselves, to themselves as well as to the society they serve; when they are not held accountable by themselves and are not constantly urged to examine their presuppositions, their processes and acts, they stiffen up and lose their evolving complementarity to other American institutions.

I believe, for reasons set forth in this volume, that since the end of World War II and the Korean War, America's colleges and universities have failed in these terms. They have failed to reexamine their norms, natures, and roles in a period of immense change. As a result, they have failed to reeducate the public, whose goodwill and support are crucial to higher education's very existence, as to the nature of higher education—what it is for, where it fits the country's historical and current needs, what it alone cannot do.

This failure to redefine and reassert itself, to be accountable or even appear to be accountable—either because of smugness or of a failure of nerve or, as I suggest in "The Academic Mission," of a desire to mimic government or the for-profit corporation—has had two results. The first is that a vacuum of definition and public education about the nature of higher education has occurred for a generation. And into that vacuum left by higher education's leaders have rushed all manner of fatuous or reactionary critical accounts of higher education's mission, explanations whose surface plausibility and essential wrongheadedness have found a willing and eager national audience, hungry to know what has been going on. The critiques, rarely encountering an institutionally generated countervailing point of view, colonize the vacuum created and maintained by higher education about itself.

A parent who hungers to know, for instance, why a child's college experience has cost so much or, worse, has seemed so unsatisfactory or pointless or lacking in connectedness with anything in the past will have heard very little from higher education about its issues or its problems. Certainly, that parent will not hear a voice like that of a Conant or a Hutchins or a Griswold against which to test one's ideas, to argue, with which to agree. Small wonder that Allan Bloom's book is a best-seller. There is no impedance in the atmosphere; no one to assert how higher education in fact serves a democracy not by re-creating a class of micro-mandarins, strenuously emulating Socrates, but rather by maintaining faith with a national history that at its best aches for equality as well as quality, for accessibility as well as excellence.

Most of the voices one hears tend to be those announcing the Apocalypse. Few are the assertions for the public at large of the ideals to which higher education must aspire, few are the assertions of the shape an institution of higher education must attain and why, and few are the consistent visions of the purpose of an undergraduate education. In the last generation, the field has been, with few exceptions, left to the promoters of a political system or of lament. When those who know best the realities and the ideals of higher education fall silent, for whatever reason, or believe themselves only managers, not leaders, then the public is denied access to higher education in a fundamental sense, access to its thinking about what is going on and what it is for.

The other result of a generation of silence concerning the principles and purposes of higher education has been the absence of any examination of a college's or a university's necessary complementarity with the other institutions in our society. We all know that the basic institution in society—the family—has changed its shape; we know that the legal system, and the services it absorbs or spawns, has undergone great change because of a different set of demands placed upon it. We know that institutions for worship have adapted to new technologies, new populations with differing needs, and new imperatives; that cultural institutions, and institutions for leisure, have changed to meet a population whose patterns of work, play, and retirement are different from what they were before 1950. And we know there is even a portion of the population that does not believe in the traditional institution, and its authority, at all; for these people, all traditional institutions are sexist plots or capitalist instruments designed to deny Rights and Freedoms. Such people are found (among other places) in the student bodies and faculties of many colleges and universities. While their essentially redistributionist and leveling impulses, vaguely compounded of New Left, Old Left, and narcissistic postures, hardly represent more than a fraction of any campus, hardly more than a special flavor to various Special Interests, they do—paradoxically—impede the process of institutional redefinition by baying so stridently for radical change that they spark counterreformations that invariably go back to the recoverable past for their counterproposals.

The net effect since the Second World War is that institutions of higher education have lost vital connections to their surrounding institutions. Universities and colleges have tended to lurch into new structures and programs, with no thought of consequences, and then spastically to reinstitute what had been jettisoned in a new, watered-down form. Educational institutions are out of phase with themselves as well, because there are few voices reminding them of how many times they have been through this cycle and, more important, redefining and remembering for each generation the enduring principles and purposes of the place. Only by those affirmations can the change that is essential to the institution within occur; and only by such change within does the university remain in phase, in a complementary relationship, with the changing institutions around it.

When the university lurches spasmodically rather than changes in a patient, inefficient, but purposeful way, a larger society that hears nothing about the principles and purposes of higher education from clear voices within higher education also sees the whole class of institutions as floundering, as growing more expensive when costs supposedly are going down; as abdicating the role of *in loco parentis* just when the family is under increasing stress; as asking more and more of government (while wishing to be independent) just when government, at the federal level in particular, is arguing for a New Federalism and a less intrusive (and supportive) federal role; as seemingly indifferent to drugs or drinking just when the public grows in awareness of the evils of substance abuse.

A clear instance: the central cry, heard on all sides, is, Why don't our colleges teach "moral values"? The cry is cried out constantly, and not only from outside the Academy. And here we come full circle. Without anyone clearly and forthrightly telling students and their parents (and everyone else) that a college or university teaches "moral values" by its *acts as an institution,* by its institutional behavior, and not by causing some dogma or doctrine to be propounded exclusively in its classrooms, there is no education of the public, or the academic world, regarding the nature of the modern, nonsectarian American college or university. Silence does not make the point that families are where moral values (or immoral values) are first and longest implanted; that churches or synagogues or other houses of worship are where moral values are supposed to be taught; and that the classroom, or the academic part of the university, is where values of all kinds are meant to collide, to contest, to be tested, debated, disagreed about—freely, openly, civilly (as opposed to coercively). Silence does not assert that institutional behavior—how the university or college treats the people within it, invests its money, admits students, promotes faculty, comports itself vis-à-vis other social institutions—is every day, in a thousand different forms, how the college or university teaches. The place teaches by example. In this fashion, it is a model for ethical or moral behavior or it is not, but however it acts, people—within and without—draw lessons.

Silence about the nature and purpose of higher education will never remind those who have forgotten or inform those who never knew. Nor will silence from higher education convince any member of the public at large that colleges and universities understand their necessary and complementary relationship to other institutions in the society.

➤➤ Part One

THE NATURE
AND PURPOSE OF
THE UNIVERSITY

⟫ The Academic Mission ⟪

"The Americans," said Tocqueville, "have combated by free institutions the tendency of equality to keep men asunder, and they have subdued it" (II, chap. 4). So said the French visitor who saw into our national soul in the 1830s.

He was struck again and again by how the institutions for education and for religion played a central role in containing a practical, energetic, disparate, materialistic people. He once wrote to a friend in Paris,

> . . . The effort made in this country to spread instruction is truly prodigious. The universal and sincere faith that they profess here in the efficaciousness of education seems to me one of the most remarkable features of America,

First delivered, in different form, before the Association of School Administrators, New Orleans, February 1987, and then, in revised form, as the commencement address at Franklin and Marshall College, Lancaster, Pennsylvania, May 1987.

the more so as I confess that for me the question is not yet entirely decided. But it is absolutely clear in the minds of the Americans, whatever their opinions political or religious. The Catholic himself in this matter gives his hand to the Unitarian and the Deist. Thence results one of those powerful efforts, quiet but irresistible, that nations sometimes make when they march toward a goal with a common and universal impulse.*

That sincere faith in education has not waned in the one hundred and fifty years since Tocqueville, nor has the capacity of free institutions to keep us cohesive been replaced by anything better. But for the last twenty years, the American people's faith in the institutions of education has been waning. The people are dismayed by what they believe to be a widening gap between promise and performance, between what the schools and the means for education (at any level) say they do and what the people believe they in fact do. The plethora of commission reports, white papers, books, and critiques of public education at the secondary level is a symptom of this eroded faith. But the ultimate object of that grass-roots dissatisfaction is not the public high schools; it is the nation's colleges and universities.

I do not mean there is a conscious plot on anyone's part to challenge higher education. I mean that since the late sixties, when colleges were viewed as incoherent, preaching to the nation and unable or unwilling to manage themselves at the same time, and since the late seventies,

---

* G. W. Pierson, *Tocqueville in America*, abridged by D. C. Lunt from *Tocqueville and Beaumont in America* (Garden City, N.Y.: Doubleday, 1959), p. 294.

when tuitions spiraled up as general inflation began to level and come down, the middle class has wondered if it is all worth it. Do these places only preach and never perform? Are they havens for the trivial pursuits of the privileged, or do they still teach necessary skills, some sense of tradition, some values that are recognizable? Is the commercialization of "students" in athletics for revenue really a legitimate function of a university? In short, is this historically valued way of entering American society, this means to making yourself into someone who can be productive as a person and useful as a citizen—a college education—really worth it? Or has the system become so concerned with its own squabbles and perquisites and weird forms of job security, so obsessed with maintaining itself as a system, that it is beyond accountability and not worth the tremendous investment it constantly requires? And the question beneath all the questions is, What is the purpose of your college or university? You have not told us, educators and administrators, and we can no longer see or know the point.

American institutions of higher education have been so busy managing the assaults of McCarthyism and then the upheavals of Civil Rights, the Vietnam War, and the youth movement, so busy coping with demographic decline, a savage inflation, and the multiple demands of multiple constituencies, including vast changes in internal governance and the need to run the business parts of themselves like businesses, that they have not since the end of World War II and the Korean War redefined themselves. Historically, after periods of national upheaval or depression, higher education has found or thrust forward a few voices who redefined the academic mission, repositioned the academy in a changed world, spoke to altered or recomposing circumstances. That has not happened in the last thirty-five years. American institutions in general and those for higher education in particular have been coping, but they have not adapted to changing times, and they are no longer perceived as leading. They are not perceived as leading, because, in fact, the institutions themselves, while being competently managed in most cases, are not necessarily themselves being led.

Management is the capacity to handle multiple problems, neutralize various constituencies, motivate personnel; in a college or university, it means hitting as well the actual budget at break-even. Leadership, on the other hand, is an essentially moral act, not—as in most management—an essentially protective act. It is the assertion of a vision, not simply the exercise of a style: the moral courage to assert a vision of the institution in the future and the intellectual energy to persuade the community or the culture of the wisdom and validity of the vision. It is to make the vision practicable, and compelling.

A college or university is an institution where financial incentives to excellence are absent, where the product line is not a unit or an object but rather a value-laden and life-long process; where the goal of the enterprise is not growth or market share but intellectual excellence; not profit or proprietary rights but the free good of knowledge; not efficiency of operation but equity of treatment; not increased productivity in economic terms but increased intensity of thinking about who we are and how we live and about the world around us. In such an institution, leadership is much more a rhetorical than a fiscal or "strategic" act. While never denigrating the day-to-day, never scorning the legitimate and difficult chores of management, never pretending that efficiency is useless or productivity irrelevant, leadership in such an institution must define institutional shape, that is, define its standards and purposes—define the coherent, sustainable, daring, shared effort of learning that will increase a given community's freedom, intellectual excellence, human dignity.

Such assertions of leadership—by speech, by deed, through decisions large and small—are the essential acts of institutional definition. And because in the last generation such compelling acts of institutional definition have been largely unarticulated, there is very little consensus about what the role of a given campus or its programs is, about what higher education is for and how it connects with secondary education, about what a pluralistic system of higher education can do or why it is valuable. There have been few tough-minded, visionary statements or sustained assertions of how a given campus, or higher education in all its diversity, should be engaging the legitimate public questions (for instance) of access and selectivity; of equity in treatment and excellence in standards; of vocational training and general education in values; of curricular reform, and to what end; of remedial needs and the quest for rigor; of service to a local or state community—its public schools, its need for continuing education, its economic viability—and focus on the individual need for intellectual growth and ethical awareness. We hear of the tactics and strategy for this institution or that, but rarely if ever of the nature and purpose of a college: What is it for? How is an academic institution different from a government or a for-profit corporation? Why is it important that a college or university be different? What is the price paid when those differences disappear?

The most pressing need in higher education in the next

ten years is not for management strategies. It is for debate on each campus, led by its leaders, as to what the purposes and goals of each campus are—for only in the open arrival at some shared consensus of what the contour, the shape, the tendency, of the campus or of higher education will be can the drift of American higher education be halted; can the further internal fragmentation of campuses be forestalled; can the rush to special interest be reversed; can the public's faith that these places know what they are about, know why they exist and where they are going, be restored.

Because the history of higher education in the United States has since the eighteenth century been a history of public initiatives, of federal encouragement and support for education, the classic tension in American culture between structures meant to express the general will and to protect the individual right is also visible in the history of higher education. Thus, when the public begins to be distrustful of institutions of higher education, that distrust manifests itself in the relationship between institutions of higher learning and the federal government, which has been both a source of support and a center of antagonism. At present, we are in a period when the antagonistic feeling between institutions of higher learning and the federal government has reached an extraordinary pitch.

This unhealthy situation is the necessary context within which to understand three general changes moving across universities, and where, therefore, higher education may go for the rest of this century. All the changes stem from the Second World War; all have as their background the presence of the federal government and of local institutions for higher education, on the one hand, and the attitude of the general public, on the other hand. In putting the issues that way, I have projected a context that is typically academic, because I have placed the question in terms that make it sound as if academic people and academic institutions in the United States were constantly under siege, one of the most cherished myths of American academic people. The sense of feeling marginal, the sense of being peripheral, the sense therefore of being legitimatized to become a priestly caste, is one of the most stimulating feelings that American academics in the absence of other feelings have. I want you to understand that I am aware that the very terms in which I put the issues reflect the biases that may be examples of the problem.

The first of the three movements I wish to note briefly is what I would call the codification of the academy, which occurs when codes displace those values traditionally viewed as collegial. Collegiality is the shared sense of a shared set of values, values about open access to information, about open exchange of ideas, about academic freedom, about openness of communication and caring; collegiality is the shared belief, regardless of field or discipline, in a generalized, coherent, communal set of attitudes that are collaborative and intellectual. It does not imply unanimity of opinion; it implies commonality of assumption. Collegiality is the most precious asset in any institution of learning, and it is precious to the extent to which it is, if not unspoken, at least unwritten. At its worst, collegiality is a kind of clubbiness, an impulse to exclusivity; at its best, it is a genuinely vital sense of community. Collegiality at its best, which I would define as the most remarkable asset in nontangible form any institution of higher learning can nourish and cherish within itself, is precisely what is damaged when one moves from making these personal relationships a matter of shared belief to making them forms of public expression.

In the last fifteen years, under the pressure of thousands of pages, following millions of dollars, of government regulations, those private values have been forced to find public expression. All written codes for grievance procedures, for admission procedure, for promotion procedure, for affirmative action—the elaborate codes that now inhabit all American campuses for the assessment of everything from racial, religious, and ethnic insensitivity to the assurance of intellectual quality and human equity are a form of codification. As soon as you make something explicit in language, you risk losing those values you intended to save. The gain is that privacy, exclusivity, and discrimination give way to rules that are public, more procedurally open, more juridically sound. The loss is that the texture, the feeling, of sharing is now displaced by the legal mandate to share. In this collision of values between something that is unspoken and something that is written, more is gained than lost, more good results than bad. American universities are now almost in fact as accessible and open as they always said they were. That is a development I applaud. But in applauding it, one must not be blind to the reality that in the reductions to language and rule making something that is precisely beyond language is lost. The impulse to write things down, and to formalize every process that once upon a time was unspoken, will go on, and I think ought to go on. But at a cost. Nothing comes for nothing, said Emerson.

The second movement goes along with this. I would

call it the corporatizing of the American university. One of the great inventions of America in the twentieth century has been the private corporation as an entity and as a style of management. I do not know very much about American corporations. I do know, however, that one of the tensions in American culture has been between the private, proprietary corporation, whose norms are competition, efficiency, and "profit maximization," and whose goals are short-term, and the traditional university, which is nonprofit and whose goals are intellectual, civic, and long-term. Since the Second World War, the management style of the American corporation has begun to encroach upon the ecclesiastical style of the university. And that has been a very difficult transition. You will find universities that ten years ago were run in a collegial fashion now completely structured to look from the outside as if they were manufacturing or banking firms, with tables of organization replete with executive vice-presidents, vice-presidents, lawyers: all the appurtenances of a major profit-making corporation. This has been thought on the whole to be a wonderful thing. I do not necessarily think it is a wonderful thing at all, but in that I reflect a bias that is much more comfortable with the older, ecclesiastical-like hierarchial structure of the American university than with the more modern, management structure.

American universities in the nineteenth century took a German research-oriented structure, grafted it to older- (English) style residential colleges, democratized its values, and created an independent, research-oriented collegiate institution that did not look like anything else. At a certain moment in our time, the American corporation began to make the point that until universities managed their nonacademic part in a fashion that corresponded with the successful corporate structure, they would not be helpful or useful to higher education. There ensued the gradual encroachment of the corporate management structure into the American university. It has made the university more prudentially sound and has made it somewhat more efficient. But this implantation of a corporate management style has also made the academy more distrustful than ever of the graft it has engaged. And when you add to the new corporate management structure the traditional academic distrust of the corporate world, then you have a very interesting situation: the reawakened mistrust of the corporation in the academy occurs in the academy that has now begun to look more like a corporation. All of this at the very same moment when the private corporation is being urged by the government to become a source for research money that the government will no longer provide.

These two movements—codifying and corporatizing—are both destructive of collegiality in the sense that they presume to reduce all intellectual and moral issues to precise language or to management solutions sought by organizing a structure. The result is the third movement or challenge to higher education—the splitting off of the faculty from the administration. American university faculties, in research institutions in particular, are more and more being driven both by internal and by external forces to see themselves as the bearers of values, and university administrations to see themselves as the bearers of law. The traditional view of academic people in America—as people for whom the law and the values were coincident, for whom there was no gap, for whom a life of research, a life of teaching, and a decent human existence were all at one—may have been a myth, may have been an illusion, but it was one of those wholly nourishing illusions by which we all live and which nourish a nonprofit life.

Now the faculty and the administration are split by governmental regulation. People of the kind I was, little ceremonial objects, are obliged under the law, rightly, to sustain, support, and if not defend at least promulgate, regulatory impulses, rules, that grow from the federal government or from within the institutions as if the college or university were a government. And we are often at variance with the very values of the faculty that we continue to assert or to maintain. The problem in the long run will make two worlds within the one world of the university: it will split universities into management and labor in ways no NLRB or union could do. University professors never think of themselves as employees; they think of themselves as the heart of the place, as the texture of the place, as the essence of the place. And they are right. Since the nineteenth century, the statutes of Yale styled the full professors as the "permanent officers." I was an impermanent officer as the president; only as a professor was I a permanent officer of the university. Therefore, to make the permanent officers responsible for values but not for process, to make administrators responsible for rules but not for spirit, is to split things apart that in fact should not be split, lest the institutions be put asunder.

What I fear the most in the universities and colleges in America is that those who are responsible for the legal processes and those who are responsible for the daily life of the mind will see themselves as somehow engaged in different things. I fear we will come to the point where the corporate structure will take over, where presidents, deans, chancellors, and lawyers will be constantly negotiating with the court on the one hand and with the faculty on the other. When that happens, one of the great changes will have occurred in the American universities. Such changes occur, as they do in most human institutions that go back in time, once every sixty or seventy years. We will have moved the university into a model that is much more the corporate enterprise, accustomed to long-range planning for short-term goals; we will have made the university another product of an industrial society instead of the ethical center by which culture is transmitted and in which independent thinking is done.

When administrators believe themselves only managers of the public policy of the place and faculty members believe themselves alone in guarding the flame of intellectual values, when presidents and deans on the one hand and members of the faculty on the other may even question whether they share the same goals, the same mission, the same hopes, then they split apart. They speak of US and THEM. They begin to replace the choreography of administrative/faculty competition—balletic in its precision—with the dug-in passion of true adversaries. That atmosphere has been growing for about fifteen years on America's campuses. It is subtle, and dangerous. No institution for teaching and learning can survive it.

No less dangerous, if far less subtle, is the atmosphere on so many campuses caused by the voices of the Moral Minority, the voices that for every cause—social, political, academic, sexual, religious, or ethnic—demand satisfaction, NOW. These voices are scornful of complexity, indifferent to ambiguity, contemptuous of competitive views or values. They are the enemies of give-and-take, of the open conversation that is the process of education. Hungering for Decree, for Absolutes, these voices are encouraged because they are said to be "idealistic." What they are is precisely not idealistic, but, in their simplifying, reductionistic. These voices are the worst enemies the college or university could have because they wish to freeze what is by nature fluid, and they invariably and inevitably create a counterreaction they cannot handle or resist. By then conversation, the conversation that is free and open, has ceased.

It is that civil conversation—tough, open, principled—between and among all members and parts of the institution that must be preserved. If it is, a community is patiently built. If it is not, the place degenerates into a center of crisis management and competing special interests. What must be open and free is the conversation, between young and young, young and old, scholar and scholar, present and past—the sound of voices straining out the truth.

American colleges and universities do not play the role in our society as centers for independent thought, for the open pursuit of truth, for the protection of minority or dissenting or critical views—they do not serve America—when they mimic governmental institutions or private businesses or allow themselves to be simply holding pens for competing dogmas. American colleges and universities serve neither themselves nor the country if they are unsure of their own principles and purposes or if they cannot convey them to the people at large. The deepest need is for the permanent parts of the place—the members of the faculty and the administration—to reforge common aims, to establish again a common set of goals and values, to lay aside the mistrust that corrodes the capacity to educate the young and to discover and share new knowledge, and to speak to the public of the nature and purpose of an education.

To be able to train the next generations in the liberal arts and sciences—that is, in the disciplines for knowledge that teach the mind to free itself—in order freely to pursue the truth, the institutions of higher education in America must themselves be shapely, free, and ordered, places with a moral and intellectual contour, or they will not be able to teach the interplay of freedom and order that shapes an individual or a society. If there is a vision we press for, let it be of our nation's schools and colleges as free and ordered spaces, for those who live there, for the country at large; let the institutions for education be strong in their vision of themselves as both a source and a symbol for the freely inquiring mind, supportive of the right of other minds freely to inquire. Let this be our common vision for our schools; let this be, as Tocqueville said, the goal of our common and universal impulse.

⫸ *The Nature and Purpose of the University* ⫷

A civilized order is the precondition of freedom, and freedom of belief, speech, and choice—the goal of responsible order. A university cannot expound those goals and expect a larger society to find them compelling, it cannot become a repository of national hope and a source of national leadership, unless it strives to practice what it teaches. If its goals are noble, so must be its acts.

The American university constantly challenges the capacity of individuals to associate in a spirit of free inquiry, with a decent respect for the opinion of others. Its values are those of free, rational, and humane investigation and behavior. Its faith, constantly renewed and ever vulnerable, holds that if its values are sufficiently respected within, their growth will be encouraged without. Its purpose is to teach those who wish to learn, to learn from those it teaches, to foster research and original thought, and,

Inaugural address, October 1978.

> 47 <

through its students and faculty, to disseminate knowledge and to transmit values of responsible civic and intellectual behavior. That purpose can never become the captive of any single ideology or dogma. Nor can it be taken for granted.

In its purpose, the University embodies the pluralistic spirit of America, and it embodies that spirit in another way as well. The country's promise that diverse peoples, with diverse origins and goals, can compete on the basis of merit for the fulfillment of their aspirations is also the basic premise of the University's composition. But while the University engages the best hopes and, at various stages, the ablest people of the larger society, it does not pretend in every respect to be a microcosm of the larger society. While it has democratized its values, it has not in every sense made its structure democratic. The University's structure is a hierarchy unlike any other; it is neither military nor corporate, nor is it even a hierarchy like the Church, whence sprang the earliest University teachers. With its instincts for collaboration and its strategies for consultation, the University is finally a patient and persuasive hierarchy, designed to cherish a particular value-laden process and the individuals within it. That process is, of course, the educational process, wherein the individual, often alone, often with others, seeks constantly to clarify limits in order to surpass them, constantly seeks to order the mind so as to set it free. That seeking is the University's essence.

Intellectual and civic in nature, pluralistic in purpose and composition, hierarchical in structure, the University exists for that play of restraint and release in each of its individual members. Through that creative play of opposites in teaching, learning, and research, the University ✦ nourishes at its core the humanizing and spacious acts of the individual imagination. Those acts are found in every area of study, whether lasers, literature, or law, and are proof of the human capacity to make and to impose a design. Those designs made by the imagination are the signs of our ability to shape instinct and flux, to find or reveal patterns in the seemingly unplanned. The University is the guardian of the imagination that both defines and asserts our humanity.

The University is not only the guardian of that human capacity; it is also its triumph. For as the University is devoted to fostering these individual acts of imagination, so the University is an imaginative act in itself. In its mixed structure, its assertions about itself, its mingled character as a force for change and a wellspring of continuity, the University is in a sense self-consciously artificial. The University is something made, not born, cradling those individual acts of shaping that it figures forth. It is our culture's assertion that what is made by the mind has value and can convey values. Thus the University, rooted in history, open to every new impulse, insists on its centrality to culture and on its uniqueness. Thus it is so powerful and so fragile, the foe of the merely random, insistent on order while urging freedom, convinced that the human mind, out of nature, can fashion shapes and patterns nature never bore, and convinced that it is prime among the artifacts.

Where universities, or those within them, falter is in believing that the formal nature of the University, what I have called its artificial character, necessarily removes them and their inhabitants from the common stream of society; that because universities assert the mind's capacity, in the best sense, to contrive, they can condescend to or smugly disdain whatever is not encompassed by them. Such an attitude has brought many institutions the scorn they deserve, for they have chosen to be sanctuaries from society and not tributaries to it. To wish only to be removed from the culture, and not to be part of its renewal, is to long for the atrophy, not the exercise, of the imagination and its works. I return to where I began—no university is strong if it is unsure of its purpose and nature, and is unwilling or unable to make vital that nature and purpose for others beyond it. We lose our public trust when we treat as only private our principal obligations.

Only when we clarify what we believe are the larger values, and value, of a private education can we expect that education to have a significant effect for the public good. Yale's basic strength derives from our common sense of what we do, why we do it, and whom we mean to reach.

Our strength also derives from our capacity to know where our problems will occur. While no Sybil has yet vouchsafed me certain knowledge of the future, even one unencumbered by special vision can see the outlines of our path. Let me review what is perhaps known to all here, and then speak of some particular challenges before us.

Earlier this fall, I had occasion to note a mood of closure and withdrawal that seems to be growing around us. I sense more than the contraction and spasm of isolation that would inevitably follow a period as expansive as the sixties and an experience as searing as the war in Vietnam. This mood of disaffiliation has these roots and others as well, and it casts a longer shadow. We are coming to the end of the twentieth century, and the knowledge we bear weighs heavily. Part of our knowledge is the realization that systems, technological and ideological, in which we had such faith, have their limits, that we may have reached those limits, and that we are being left with only the fragments of our hopes. We are closing not only a century but also a millennium, and the accumulated force of that realization heightens a certain apocalyptic impulse, a febrile fatigue. As if to accommodate this spirit and contain it, the country seems to want to settle only for a credible competence in its education, its government, its means of pleasure, its craftsmanship. It should never want less, but it ought to aspire to more, and universities and colleges must have the will and the energy to focus themselves, and the nation, on renewal despite the entropy that a sense of closure creates. Because the next years in our enterprise of education will be difficult, because nothing one can see will make them easy, our faith in ourselves and our courage to do what we believe in must be all the stronger. Let me be specific.

General economic conditions, specifically a corrosive inflation, will place educational institutions, with their concentrations of people, increasingly on the defensive. These institutions will be harder pressed than ever to retain their levels of financial aid, to keep tuitions from escalating at anything less than the national rate of inflation, to compensate those who work in them at levels commensurate with their skills. And those assaults of a fiscal nature will only be abetted by inevitable demographic curves. Within a dozen years, there will be just about a million fewer eighteen-year-olds in America than there were three years ago.

The competition for potential college applicants will increase dramatically, and no institution will be immune. For even those universities whose colleges will still attract a greater pool of applicants than there will be places in a class will feel this shrinkage because their doctoral candidates will find, as so many are now finding, that there is no market for their skills. Indeed, of all the immediate challenges facing the major research universities—to sustain research libraries, to support academic science in the context of a university population that will shrink, to plan the direction of medical education, to finance graduate students, and to embrace part-time or older students in new patterns—the most difficult and internally consequential will be the need to attract into the academic profession the ablest and most dedicated young men and women. Nothing that we do in colleges or universities or that the country wants done is possible without the next generation of teachers and scholars. I will return to this concern.

In the years ahead of us, precisely because the pressures on private institutions, whether large or small, old or new, will increase, it will be essential to affirm the particular character of private institutions and to remember that because times are financially strained, the government is not always the place to turn for help. Such rescue, even if it were to occur, would result in more regulation. Of course we depend on federal funds for a wide variety of crucial research and financial aid; of course there are legitimate requirements of accountability for the taxpayers' dollars that follow federal funds; of course there are legitimate regulatory functions of the federal government. But the capacity of a private institution to choose for itself what its course will be, in keeping with the law of the land, is essential to its nature and purpose, and we must be constantly wary of governmental intrusion and of asking for or accepting more. We must retain our freedom of expression and of purpose.

Private educational institutions, however, must not only resist external interference. They must realize they are an integral part of the private sector, and other portions of the private sector must also come to this realization. As I have had occasion to say, the ancient ballet of mutual antagonism—at times evidently so deeply satisfying—between private enterprise, on the one hand, and private education, on the other, is not to anyone's interest. That ballet of antagonism must give way to a capacity for responsible collaboration. There is a metaphor that informs the private business sector as it informs the private educational sector, and that is the metaphor of the free marketplace. Whether the competition of the free marketplace is of commodities or of ideas, it is a common metaphor and a precious asset.

Obviously, I am not asking to resist governmental intrusion in order to encourage or accept intrusion of any other kind from any other quarter. What I am saying is that precisely to retain our capacity to choose, and to survive as we wish to survive as a private institution, Yale and places like Yale must recognize their natural alliances with other private institutions. Such alliances must spring from a perception that all portions of the private sector—voluntary, corporate, and educational—have a common goal, in a pluralistic society, of providing alternatives to public structures and solutions.

Lastly, and this is less a problem than a challenge, we must be mindful of the community in which we live. No college or university in a city can regard its fortunes as separate from that city. The economic and cultural health of New Haven is intimately tied to Yale's health, and our future is intertwined with New Haven's. The City and the University share the same ground and over two hundred and fifty years of history. Yale cannot look at New Haven as if the City were an endless impediment, and New Haven cannot regard Yale as a smugly unresponsive savior. Neither attitude reflects reality, and the only attitude that will reflect reality is one of mutual regard and collaboration. The University must do all it can to assist the City in its development, and in those ways that it legitimately can, it will. The City must also understand that Yale's resources are limited and that Yale's first obligation is to fulfill itself as an educational institution. If Yale falters in that, the City cannot flourish. Those who chide Yale for not being primarily an agency of specific, local reforms in fact misapprehend the University's nature and purpose. That misapprehension in part is Yale's fault, but misapprehensions, of all kinds, should be dispelled if our common future is to be shaped in common.

And what are the prime imperatives for Yale's future? I think they are three.

First, Yale must use its financial and human resources prudently, imaginatively, and wisely. We must affirm those internal affiliations, among the Schools, among the Schools and the College, among Departments, that will focus on critical strengths and encourage new patterns of teaching and research to emerge. We will not be able to do everything, but what we choose to do we must do well. The purpose of the next years of budgetary contraction is to consolidate in order to preserve excellence and to maintain Yale's finest tradition—the offering of a private education for the public good. We cannot blink at the need to live within our means, but budgetary balance can and must be achieved in a way that enhances our quality, not in a way that sacrifices our quality.

Second, Yale must continue to reflect and nourish the pluralism of America. I take the diversity in this country—of peoples, of kinds of freedoms, and of humane and rational values—to be both a source of the country's strength and a vital principle in itself. To be truly a national institution, playing its educational and civic role to the fullest, Yale's texture can never be less varied and many-grained than the fabric of America itself. If Yale is to train leaders, they must come from and respond to every part of the larger society. This heterogeneity of talent and origin, experience and interest, is not achievable by simple formulae or by institutionalizing special privilege. It is done by continually seeking out, as students and faculty and staff, men and women of merit with a capacity to contribute to the fulfillment of themselves and hence of the place, and by continually urging and encouraging them to become part of Yale. This affirmative attitude is translated into action by our never wavering in our commitment to seek out these individuals as widely and diligently as possible.

Third, and I return to and close with a concern expressed earlier, Yale must expend every effort to nourish and encourage its young or nontenured faculty. The University must demonstrate its belief in them and their efforts. If it does not, it cannot expect younger faculty to believe in the institution or in their vocation. That vocation, the academic profession, and the younger teacher and scholar, most particularly in the humanities and certain social sciences, are now subjected to the savage pressures I noted earlier, the declining numbers of students, soaring costs, and diminishing number of jobs. And, I respectfully suggest, these pressures are only exacerbated by state legislation* that, in Connecticut, has recently denied private institutions the capacity to determine for themselves when faculty must retire. Here a governmental act, however well intentioned in its specific mission, has a devastating effect in areas clearly not envisaged by its proponents. With no age limit for faculty in private educational institutions, the private and public institutions are set at odds; the capacity of individuals and institutions to plan ahead is confounded at a critical time; the young person is placed in a hopeless position, with no sense of movement within and diminishing chances without. Finally, if one cannot recruit young faculty of quality, and give them some hope, there is a serious threat to our capacity to fulfill the human and moral principles of pluralism expressed in programs of affirmative action.

There are, of course, measures one can take, and my concern for the younger faculty in no way bespeaks a lack of regard for the older faculty. I use this example as a way of describing how so many of my concerns—about excellence, about resources, about diversity, about the character of a private institution—intersect in issues concerning the faculty, and particularly concerning our young colleagues. I believe the faculty is at the heart of this place, and I believe that at the heart of the faculty in a place like Yale is the teaching function. All the research we want

---

* Repealed in 1979.

to do, all the obligations we must carry as faculty, are in some sense nurtured by and are versions of that first calling, which is to teach our students. We want always to do more, but we can never do less. Nor can we ever forget that.

Surely, all of us can recall certain voices, the voices of teachers who changed the way we live our lives. I am concerned, at last, with the next generation of voices. I wish them to be as strong and confident and effective in what they do as those who came before. And they will be, if we recall our nature and our purpose and engage each other to fashion our future together.

⟫ *Schools and the Ideal of Education* ⟪

The stretching of instruction into citizenship is my theme. The nation's public schools are the arena of my concern. I believe in the central role of education in the formation and sustenance of a free and democratic nation, and I believe, therefore, in an education that has that civic goal as its end. Such a belief does not presume a preference for one kind of education over another. It rather assumes excellence as the driving energy toward the goal of a decent and productive life with others. My basic text, embodying these ideals, derives from a great book on elementary education, *Positions,* written in 1581 by the greatest of Elizabethan schoolmasters, Richard Mulcaster. The following passage sets forth the essential faith in education brought by the first settlers in the New World; it represents as its core the beliefs Jefferson would hold dear. "Education," said Mulcaster,

Delivered to a conference on Excellence in Education, Hartford, Connecticut, January 1981.

is the bringing up of one, not to live alone, but amongst others . . . whereby he shall be best able to execute those doings in life, which the state of his calling shall employ him unto, whether public abroad or private at home, according unto the direction of his country; whereunto he is born, and owes his whole service.

Public and *private* here refer to ourselves and the roles we choose for ourselves, all tending toward the enhancement of the common life we live with others. In America, the burden for that set of values, whose undergirding is a set of intellectual skills, has rested with the public school system, which is sustained by and responsive to the thousands of localities throughout the land. It is to those localities and the schools within them that I address myself, for to speak of excellence in education without some firm idea of the goal of excellence, and the historical traditions of that goal, would only compound our present confusion.

Our confusion stems from our worries about the state of our schools. It is compounded of anger, fear, and frustration and stems from our anxiety that there is in our schools across the country a situation bordering on endemic collapse.

The condition of many of the nation's elementary and high schools is worrisome enough; the conviction on the part of many Americans about the lack of quality and stability in the nation's public schools is even more worrisome. Whether the schools are as decayed as many people believe is not at all as clear as is the public's belief that the schools are a disaster.

Much of the anxiety derives from beliefs most Americans hold: that throughout our country's history school has been thought essential to a productive citizenry and stable society; that schooling is the responsibility equally of family and community; that the federal government has played a vital role in encouraging schools, from academies to land-grant universities, but that the federal government does not interfere with education at the local level, has not set up either a national school system or a national university; and that while the government, through the courts, has enforced a number of socially useful or desirable legal decisions within the schools, regarding integration of the races or freedom of belief, it has acted in accordance with the legal authority of the federal Constitution, not from a desire to impede local values or lawful local traditions or differences. Beneath the fascinating tangle of local and national obligations and prerogatives that the public schools present, there runs in America a basic belief that education in this officially secular society is an almost sacred process, a process meant to open opportunity, promote access and mobility, foster excellence, recognize merit, do all that urges Americans to make themselves productive, free, and equal.

It is when this constellation of potentially contradictory beliefs and systems is ignored that concern increases. Beneath the layers of anxiety that our schools are riddled with truancy, absenteeism, dropping out, and violence; that all the standard measures indicate a decline in the national ability to read and write and reckon; that teachers have lost their dedication and students their motivation and the whole system its quality, is the deepest anxiety: that no one is paying attention. The fear that local political leaders do nothing to assert the critical priority of the local schools, that national leaders retreat to bureaucratic bunkers or simply fail to acknowledge the plight of the schools, terrifies the people, particularly when the people know in their blood that somehow schools and education are still linked to jobs, economic growth and productivity, and a decent public order. The people believe those linkages but hear nothing about them from public officials, elected or appointed. And so the confusion grows until it is not hysterical but necessary to ask, What will happen to *all* young Americans' access to the American educational dream if the public schools fail or falter?

I think this question is one of the most pressing for our country at this century's end. I have no easy answer to it but do have an attitude toward how to approach the question. At the root of that attitude is a distinction I have made implicitly and must make explicit. That is the distinction I will argue America has long made between education and school. Although these terms and what they mean have often been bound or found together, the concepts are not necessarily synonymous. Indeed, to anticipate my argument, I believe our present confusion derives from the fact that the historical differences between the meanings of *education* and *school,* and the tension engendered by those differences, have been lost. And in losing that tension between different concepts we have been left with distinct and unconnected memories masquerading as institutions; all tension, and therefore all meaning, gone.

What are those different meanings and what was the useful, indeed necessary, tension between them? First the meanings. From the beginning of our life as a people under a single government, *education* has been the means to assert an intellectual and civic ideal. While never occurring as a term or a concept in the Declaration of Independence or in the Constitution, education nevertheless appeared to the framers of those public assertions of principle as the essential process to promote the Republic's national ideals of civic harmony, general happiness, and collective freedom. Education was the means to creating the public good.

Schools, however, are referred to in public documents from the earliest colonial period. In April 1642, the General Court of Massachusetts Bay asserted that because of "the great neglect of many parents & masters in training up their children in learning & labor, & other implyments which may be proffitable to the common wealth," there must be henceforth in every town men to teach the children "to read & understand the principles of religion & capitall lawes of this country."* The General Court could confidently mandate training in skills and values, labor and learning, because there was no fissure between schools and their larger purposes.

Five years later, the same assembly passed the first law in the New World setting up a "grammar school" in every jurisdiction of fifty householders. The stated intention of the law was to teach writing and reading so as to combat ignorance of the Scriptures, which ignorance was the "one chief project of that ould deluder, Satan." Another intention, however, obtrudes later in the act, when the purpose of schools and masters is also said to be "to instruct youth so farr as they shall be fitted for the university." There would be no University, so called, for over two hundred years, but in 1647 a coherent set of values, informing a basic system of schools, could project a limitless educational

---

* All citations, unless otherwise noted, are from *Documents in American History,* ed. Henry Steele Commager (New York: Appleton-Century-Crofts, 1949).

ideal along a continuum available to the mind, if not yet to the eye.

From the earliest days of the colonies and long past the Constitution's legal separation of Church and State, schools were the local expressions of a unified political and religious culture. They promoted the religious beliefs, which were also political beliefs, that were tightly tied to localities. The pre-Revolutionary schools and colleges lost their character only gradually as containers of unified religious and political systems of value, but they had by the turning of the eighteenth century already bequeathed to the new Republic a tradition that was to be one of America's most enduring: the tradition of local control over schools and the educational principles that animate a town or region. That tradition of local control persists to this day, although by the nineteenth century schools were no longer the vehicles for religious values but had become instruments of federal policy, expanding with the land as it opened up—now secular, aimed at utilitarian goals and the promotion of economic expansion.

This simplified sketch means that there was, during the early days of the Republic, in the terms *school* and *education,* a competing set of local and national aspirations. One can read these competing but fused aspirations into the fabulous sentence that opens Article 3 of the Northwest Ordinance, passed on July 17, 1787: "Religion, morality, and knowledge, being necessary to good government and the happiness of mankind, schools and the means of education shall forever be encouraged." This prophetic fusion of individual entities and general means, willing unity while assuming diversity, is a version of the competing ideals that shaped our nation and its life. One sees this competition and fusion again clearly when President Madison, in his second message to Congress on December 5, 1810, finds it necessary to argue for a national university by denying its national character. "Such an institution," says Madison, "though local in its legal character, would be universal in its beneficial effects."* Madison emphasizes the particular, not the general, character of a national, not a local, entity.

In Madison's argument for a local national school with universal benefits, he combines, by an act of rhetorical will, inherently different concepts for the public good and the local autonomy. In this willed fusion of competing theories, we recognize the outlines of the tension between education and school first hinted at in the third article of the Northwest Ordinance, and expressed at its largest in the tension between potent assertions of principle regarding all of humankind and a radical belief in the unique essence and prerogatives of the individual. The management of this larger tension is our history: in terms of our topic, historically, it means that education is a civilizing process for the general good and school is the local expression of specific, utilitarian needs, and that these concepts ought to go together even if they do not go easily.

Our present-day confusion about our schools and the role of an education does not occur, I believe, because we have resolved this tension. It occurs because we have lost the tension. We have lost it by allowing the utilitarian view of school to displace the larger educational perspective. In losing it, we have lost touch with our past, with

* Cited in an excellent study by George N. Rainsford, *Congress and Higher Education in the Nineteenth Century* (Knoxville: University of Tennessee Press, 1972), p. 20.

the fructifying energy that the older tension, fully embraced, could inspire. We have lost the will to keep a civil ideal and a utilitarian entity together in balance, and thus we have ensured the success of neither one nor the other. Schools now do not educate, we are told, nor do they prepare people to be employed; they neither promote a civic regard for the values of the larger society nor adequately prepare individuals to be working or employable adults. Without a larger educational ethic, the school is treated only as a machine, churning out an unemployable product, and is inevitably perceived as another failure of an industrialized society.

Yet, where it is seen as having failed most, in the inner city, the public school can afford least to fail. The American educational dream, after all, is no secret. That educational dream is most bitterly recalled precisely where America's most recent immigrants and longest oppressed are gathered. There the basic American educational ideal must be most alive, and it is not. This country, however, cannot turn its back on its poor and jobless; it cannot think that its ideals of equal opportunity and social mobility are too difficult to implant or cultivate among the urban or migrant poor. America cannot either by denial or by deferral allow itself to transform the public schools into warehouses for the angry or staging areas for anarchy. There must be a commitment to keep the tension between values and utility alive, so that hope will inspire information and the promise of access will elevate utility. American history and its promises, formed through our schools and means of education, cannot be denied to any of our people, lest our society rot with the failure to bring its professions of hope for all into conjunction with its daily reality.

Let us look back at some documents of our public life for a moment, not to study the nostalgias but to regather the complexity of willed beliefs and complementary tensions that formed our practical vision of civility. My intention is briefly to explore the meaning of the language of the third article of the Northwest Ordinance, that good government and the happiness of mankind must be encouraged not only through the promotion of schools but by the means of education as well. I choose three texts, from three different periods of our history, by three very different authors.

TEXT I. 1848. Horace Mann, Secretary of the Massachusetts State Board of Education, in his twelfth annual report. In the land of Emerson, the lyceum movement, and Brook Farm, Mann is imbued with a utopian idealism; he believes that in a society riven by economic and social inequality, a leaden reality can be transmuted to a golden egalitarianism by the touchstone of universal public education. He notes the wide disparity in his time and place of the rich and poor; he asks if "competence can displace pauperism," and he answers that only "universal education can counterwork this tendency to the domination of capital and the servility of labor."

Education then, beyond all other devices of human origin, is a great equalizer of the conditions of men,—the balance wheel of the social machinery. I do not here mean that it so elevates the moral nature as to make men disdain and abhor the oppression of their fellow men. This idea pertains to another of its attributes. But I mean that it gives each man the independence and the means by which he can resist the selfishness of other men. It does better than to disarm the poor of their hostility toward the rich: it prevents being poor.

This practical Transcendentalism envisions a world ultimately made secure and moral by education because it initially envisions schooling as minting the ore of the mind.

That political economy, therefore, which busies itself about capital and labor, supply and demand, interests and rents, favorable and unfavorable balances of trade, but leaves out of account the elements of a wide-spread mental development, is naught but stupendous folly.

Public schooling is education for civility because it prepares one for fruitful and productive work, and work in the world is the way to dignity and equality. As shrewd as it is idealistic, Mann's vision is at the core, practical and civic, of the American educational dream.

TEXT II. January 28, 1915. President Wilson vetoing, as Presidents Cleveland and Taft had before him, an act of Congress requiring literacy tests for new immigrants. (The act would pass over his veto in 1917.) Literacy is access in American society, thus through our history those negative tributes to its power: the slave codes that forbade teaching black people to read and write, the Congress's desire to prohibit access to America by millions of foreigners looking for work and a better life by requiring literacy where it could not always exist. Wilson believes this act is "a radical departure" from the principles and tradition of the nation.

It seeks to all but close entirely the gates of asylum which have always been open to those who could find nowhere else the right and opportunity of constitutional agitation for what they conceived to be the natural and inalienable rights of men; and it excludes those to whom the opportunities of elementary education have been denied, without regard to their character, their purposes, or their natural capacity.

Access to America denied because literacy is absent means that

> [t]hose who come seeking opportunity are not to be admitted unless they have already had one of the chief of the opportunities they seek, the opportunity of education.

For Wilson, education is one of the prime opportunities promised by America, not a prerequisite for opportunity in America. As for Mann, so for Wilson but on a broader scale, educational opportunity defines America and is the means by which to make oneself an American.

TEXT III. 1940. Associate Justice Felix Frankfurter in the case of *Minersville School District* v. *Gobitis*. The Gobitis children had been expelled from public school in Pennsylvania for refusing, according to their principles as Jehovah's Witnesses, to salute the flag. Their father sued to enjoin the Minersville school board from requiring a salute to the flag as part of school, and the district and circuit courts found for Mr. Gobitis. Frankfurter reversed the lower courts. In his opinion in 1940, however, one finds a moving affirmation of what we first noticed: the power of the school context and the educational process to unify a polity and to preserve the individual—that quintessentially American act of the will that fuses public values and private integrity in a circuit of mutual responsibility, with education at the center.

First, Frankfurter asserts, through the symbol of the flag, the larger values of society:

> The ultimate foundation of a free society is the binding ties of cohesive sentiment. Such a sentiment is fostered by all those agencies of the mind and spirit which may serve to gather up the traditions of a people, transmit them from generation to generation, and thereby create that continuity of a treasured common life which constitutes a civilization.

One may infer that not only the flag but the schoolroom as well—when more than simply schooling occurs—also contains and continues the treasured common life that constitutes a civilization. Frankfurter then turns from the society's binding values to the rights of individuals, here figured as states or school boards and, by implication, private persons:

> The precise issue, then, for us to decide is whether the legislatures of the various states and the authorities in a thousand counties and school districts of this country are barred from determining the appropriateness of various means to evoke that unifying sentiment without which there can ultimately be no liberties, civil or religious.

He returns at the end of his meditation, in a long paragraph, to a comprehensive view of the ordered society and of the individual's liberty, a view and paragraph where conceptually and structurally the educational process is placed between society and the individual, at the center:

The preciousness of the family relation, the authority and independence which give dignity to parenthood, indeed the enjoyment of all freedom, presupposes the kind of ordered society which is summarized by our flag. A society which is dedicated to the preservation of these ultimate values of civilization may in self-protection utilize the educational process for inculcating those almost unconscious feelings which bind men together in a comprehending loyalty, whatever may be their lesser differences and difficulties. That is to say, the process may be utilized as long as men's right to believe as they please, to win others to their way of belief, and their right to assemble in their chosen places of worship for the devotional ceremonies of their faith, are all fully respected.

This willed harmony between the larger public good and the sacred individual liberties, a harmony embodied in and nourished by the educational process, is the challenge—difficult, delicate, requiring constant effort—of the American educational dream that must be realized in the schools. In their differing ways, Mann, Wilson, and Frankfurter all believe education is an intangible but definable assertion of moral courage that turns schooling into civilization. In that moral act is the willed assertion that says a polity must be made through a process that is not merely political; in it is a belief in the continuous transmission of values without the imposition of a specific religious belief. In it is a voluntary assent to the binding proposition that individual freedoms must be directed to a general order that alone will preserve those freedoms. Education has been the training for this multiple act of will and belief and consent, and, in terms of our history, education has been one of our chief means of preserving the willed act that is America.

When confronted with competing and confusing pressures, we Americans always return to those original assertions of principle that first managed our tensions and taught us to measure our several freedoms and greater order. It is time to recollect again the parts of that vision, for when we ask what shall be done about our public schools, we are asking what shall be done about the future of our country. And before the numbering of programs and policies, entitlements and amendments and appropriations, begins; before we slay forests to promote more of a paper thicket of memos, mandates, and moans, let us reassert the recollected vision: that education is first the responsibility of the family, and of the householders with or without children in the schools, and of the teachers, and of the local boards, all working together, no one assuming that the others can bear such a responsibility alone.

Before we allow political leaders, wherever they are, to fall silent and turn from the intractable problems, let us remind them that some responsible voice must urge values from the center on behalf of the people, values that assert the primary importance of quality in instruction and equality of opportunity in our schools, for without that voice the schools will have no tendency, no larger, enlarging civic mission.

Before more policies and programmatic initiatives sweep over us, let us remember that the partnership of parents and neighbors, civic leaders and politicians, must first agree that the schools are the most important single asset the community holds in common. Let us assert that the duty of that partnership at home is to decide that the first priority for public money, through taxes and bonds, is the school system. And let us then insist that the partners insist that schools have a role and obligation in the treasured common life beyond mere schooling.

And when we have reassembled a vision of the purpose of school and of the means of education, then we can pass to the rebuilding of what is both a system and a process of civility. To lament only, or to paper over the cracks in schools with scarce dollars with no idea of the point of it all, to bring up our children to live alone, not with others, would be stupendous folly. That would be to accept the lie that we are a people without purpose and that excellence and equality cannot still be the unlimited aspiration of all our people. We must study, therefore, not the bygone simplicities or the new limits but the old complexities that made our dream a reality. Before programs and policies, we must reconnect with and revive the grand vision of our first principles and practicalities.

→» Family and University «←

The family is humanity's oldest institution. In the course of history, it has undergone great changes, and in America few as massive as those resulting from the subtle dislocations and often intangible strains imposed by the Depression and the Second World War and its aftermath. During the war, families were divided, many never to be knit up again. Other families were uprooted, and followed the war or went to where war-related industry provided jobs. Shifts in population from rural to urban centers were accelerated because of the demands of the war. Women joined the work force in great numbers and became the heads of households; traditional groupings of generations, patterns of rootedness, and the structure of the family all changed. We have as a culture been absorbing the aftershocks of these and other dislocations throughout the late fifties and the sixties. The consequences are

Delivered to the senior class as the baccalaureate address, May 1983.

a heightened sense of individuality and an increasing fragmentation of the family.

Today, as was noted at the Family Support Conference held at Yale last week, families are becoming smaller (25 percent of all families will soon have only one child), less internally cohesive, and less connected to each other. Increasingly, family support services are needed to take the place of the extended family. Fifty-two percent of all mothers with children under the age of thirteen work outside the home; it is projected that by the end of the decade the proportion will be 75 percent. One child out of five is being raised in a home headed by a single parent. The stresses on the family are immense and affect all parts of society. One heartrending indication of the fact that parents feel increasingly isolated and frustrated is the widespread incidence of child abuse (one million reported cases a year, at a conservative estimate).

When the institution of the family begins to fail to provide stable affection and nurture and a sense of continuity, young people begin to lose faith in institutions of all kinds. Individuals and groups begin to look for substitutes for the family in institutions that hitherto have extended the institution of the family but never before have been required to replace it. Now the institution of the public school is increasingly asked to provide more and more of the physical support and ethical guidance families customarily provided. The public school, however, cannot become a substitute for the family, enacting all or even most of the family's nurturing or affective roles, and continue to function as a school— that is, as a place where essential skills and civic goals are also cultivated. Ask the public school to do more than it can, and it will not succeed at doing anything well.

Ask any institution to assume all or most of the burdens historically borne by other institutions, and the result will be confusion throughout the culture. Institutions can exist in supportive partnerships in a society only if they first have some definable and clearly understood roles. When they begin to shift responsibility, we must beware lest they shed, rather than share, responsibility for our common life.

To note, as I have, some of the stresses and their consequences suffered by the institution of the family is not to ask for a return to a prewar state, for that emphatically cannot be and should not be. I rather ask for awareness, as you make the family's future, that in the mature fulfillment of your individual needs you must necessarily engage the needs of others. Indeed, I think a healthy family is one where an individual's autonomy is supported by the group, not denied by it. I also ask us to remember that what affects the family inevitably affects all the institutions in society. As it happens, the same forces that produced the fragmentation of the family fundamentally altered the institution for higher education. And the results have been similar: a loss of internal connectedness and sense of rootedness in the place on the part of students. Again, what may well have been gradual changes in institutions of higher education were accelerated by the advent and aftermath of the Second World War.

War shattered forever the complacent assumption that there was an immutable sequence of continuous years necessary for an education. Diverse patterns of attending college brought diverse populations to college during and after the war. Many, many men and women were sent for training to campuses they otherwise might never have seen or entered; many veterans returned to those campuses after the war. The result was to undermine older notions about who "belonged" where, or who was "supposed" to go to certain colleges, or to college at all. Disproven, too, were unspoken assumptions about how homogeneous a student population (or faculty) had to be in order for education to proceed effectively. Finally, the veterans, for whom intensity was instinctive, were content to engage a curriculum that bore the philosophic imprint of a prewar world, but they were deeply impatient with pedagogy that was comfortably authoritarian or with courses of study that sought to foster general knowledge and graceful skills. The veterans wanted to get to the point, specialize, and get on with life.

Experienced, mature, intellectually starved men and women, having defended time-honored values, returned to pursue traditional goals and dreams. What they had seen and done, however, forever changed what they had left behind and what they now reengaged. Hungry for stability and coherence, the almost eight million veterans were the unwitting agents of the greatest changes in higher education in this century. They changed the campuses, in atmosphere, in assumption, and in structure. Of course, because of the war, the campuses had already begun to change themselves and were receptive to what came to them after the war.

In what direction did colleges change? The changes, working themselves out in the last thirty or more years, have been away from an institution that was family-like, where everyone bore, or came to bear, a "family resemblance," where governance, curriculum, and social life collaborated to reinforce already shared values and to project traditional goals of work and leisure. They have, instead, been toward an institution more focused on academic achievement, equal opportunity, and preprofessional training, a marketplace of competing forms of merit, where merit tends to be defined as identifiable skills and potential for academic performance. In the generation since the Second World War, the American college has been shedding its communal nature and assuming a competitive one.

Insofar as the institutions of the family and of the college have been losing their sense of shared values, I lament the changes. Insofar as the institution of the college, however, has become more accessible and inclusive, I applaud the change.

Both institutions changed because of the war, though the changes in the family had more to do with causing eventual changes on campuses than vice versa. In the course of this thirty-year span occurred a five- or six-year period called the Sixties, a period of great upheaval on campuses. During the Sixties, under great pressures, the changes initiated twenty years earlier came to fruition. The Sixties was also the time when students cried out for an older, communal or family-like atmosphere and structure on campuses, the very places that no longer believed themselves to exist "in loco parentis." That desperate cry for family came from the children whose own families had borne the burden of the changes the war had wrought.

For all the gains in public awareness of social needs in the last thirty-five years, there has been a private loss, the loss of certitude about the ability of certain crucial institutions upon which we all depend to sustain us. You come at the end of a period of expansion of resources and of processes for justice and of fragmentation of faith in older certitudes. With the rest of us, you will be part of the necessary effort to re-create stable institutions and reconfigure social and personal partnerships. I believe, for example, that the American family will have to assume, again, the primary responsibility for promoting the education of the young (the unmistakable message, in the recent critiques of our public schools). I also believe that the American college will have to recall that it has some responsibility for forms of nurture and for affirming common moral values as well as for fostering intellectual prowess. These two institutions, so basic to our best hopes and our deepest pleasures, must be among others the beneficiaries of a regeneration and redefinition of obligations. Only when as individuals we restore a sense of proportion and complementarity in the obligations we place on our institutions will the institutions be able to provide the coherence and continuity we need to fulfill ourselves as individuals.

⇶ A Family of Freedoms and Responsibilities ⇷

There is no balm or soothing unguent I can offer you to allay whatever sense of apprehension you may have regarding what lies before you, save to say that what you may be experiencing is healthy and normal and will soon fade. It will be replaced by excitement and pleasure as you gradually make new friends and meet new ideas and fully realize how wise and farsighted you and Yale were in choosing each other. Your life here will become if not clear (almost nothing ever becomes clear to the inquiring mind) at least clearer. Give it time.

Having endured a summer of public cheerfulness and private moments of doubt, now still smarting pleasantly from all the admonitions and good wishes of those you left at home, you probably find yourself in the grip of a feeling compounded of tension, freedom, and giddy dismay. That feeling is called a state of independence and will

Freshman address, September 1984.

become an essential feature of your inner landscape, the terrain within, that you will cultivate and make your own as you live and learn at Yale. It is about this state of independence that I want to talk to you today.

To speak of achieving independence through your education, let me begin by remembering the summer we all have just experienced. I, at least, found it a curious summer. It was filled with television images of people competing for mastery over one another, in San Francisco, in Los Angeles, in Dallas, while simultaneously assuring us of their unity and cooperation. Whenever someone, by dint of speed or speech or some kind of strength, managed to overcome someone else, protocols of concord ensured—hands clasped, arms raised, banners and music and embraces abounding, all intertwined with moments or hours of the fiercest spiritual and physical struggle. To all three cities, delegations came, of people superb at what they do and deeply committed to winning, in each case needing the public—that is, needing to be seen in order for their efforts to have meaning. In all three cities, the public events, whether political or athletic, promoted an agreed-upon doctrine, amplified by the press, which, for those disposed to believe or be persuaded, established a deeper, richer, more complex meaning for all of life.

The two political conventions and the Olympic Games were festivals of competition and cooperation. The very combining of competition and cooperation was itself the creed being propounded: that through contention can come commonality, that by way of individual opposition can come an achievement of our general humanity. Whether everyone participating in the events believed the message each event sent forth, or even was aware of it, is beside the point. The ceremonies were vast rituals enacting the continuous search by the American people for a stable creed, a religious doctrine capacious enough to include everyone and coherent enough to provide a spiritual framework for shared values. Because no single formal religion can embrace a people who hold so many faiths, including no particular formal faith at all, sports and politics are the civil surrogates—at least this summer—for a people ever in quest for a covenant.

As I suggested, the underlying covenant or convention—the widely held common belief—at the two political gatherings and the Games was the conviction, put at its simplest, that the individual, through talent and striving, can triumph and in that single victory will somehow catch up and make manifest our capacity for common coherence. We were told and assured and told again that the Democratic or Republican or Olympic ideal was solitary struggle and diversity as the route to unity and shared humanity. In all its many permutations, this proved a compelling credo and, as we saw this summer, a cohesive one when deftly presented.

Running through the summer's propagation of this doctrine was the image and idea of family. We saw families; we heard constantly about family and family values; we even had that westernmost outpost Fort Olympic Village proffered as a miniaturized global family. The family was interviewed, invoked, prayed over, taped, and disclosed. But whether all the versions of family and meaning attached to family were real or even present, the genuine, enduring idea of the family survived all the exploitation. The image of the family bound, as it was meant to, the disparate parts into one whole, while offering an idea of how the individual is accorded the freedom to grow and go away and yet be connected to the rest of us.

At the heart of the American belief in individual initiative, in solitary striving and common responsibility, in sacred individual and shared freedoms, in consent leading to liberty leading to a civil order that guarantees liberty built on consent, is the covenant of the family. And while the idea and the reality of family may be exploited or made banal, while there is always a gap between the ideal of family and anyone's actual familial circumstances, nothing can finally lessen the power of the idea of the family or indeed lessen the sum of humanity's wisdom that tells us the family provides an irreducible and yet splendidly elastic model for the coherence of freedom and order.

And thus by a path roundabout but relevant we come back to today. You have—perhaps for the first time—now removed yourself from family at the beginning of your journey toward what I called at the outset a state of independence. The University cannot and should not, and will not, displace your family. Your family, whatever shape it takes, is and always will be yours, the first seminary of values and affection and connection. But as you grow, the University will provide other versions of family, connections of intellect in common academic pursuits; connections of shared striving in athletic and artistic and social activities; connections of shared and pleasurable daily life in the manageable, intelligible life of a dormitory or residential college. You will find, to say it all, that a state of independence is achieved by broadening your connections and affiliations, intellectual, spiritual, human.

The paradox into which one gradually grows, through education and throughout one's life, is that independence is achieved through consenting to interdependence. I believe we grow in individual liberty in this country when we recognize the human needs and rights of others. I believe a state of independence comes when we decide through our intellect and spirit to forge human connections. Without connections, there is no individual coherence. There is no independence in uprootedness; there is only drift and decay. There is no growth of the moral and mental powers of the self if the self alone is the ultimate goal of learning. Independence of an enduring kind, noble and practical, arrives only when one realizes what it means, in all its glory and responsibility, that one is not alone.

What does this mean for your new life at Yale? It means that you here enter multiple families and now begin to fashion many new affiliations of mind and spirit which, if pursued with passion for ideas and devotion to justice and reason—in a spirit tough-minded and openhearted— will lead to a state of independence. It means that you bring here whatever values were instilled in you at home, in your family; if those values, as I trust they are, are honorable and sound and deeply held, you will not lose them; you will add them, as you add yourself, to the increase of individual growth and communal connection in this place.

It means you will begin to engage the values of this academic family or group of families. The values of the Yale families are distinct and deeply rooted in our community: openness, honesty, intellectual inquiry for the truth, and mutual respect. These values foster debate, disagreement, diversity of ideas and opinions; they protect freedom of expression and the open exchange of ideas, because that is the essence of a free, independent university in a democracy. We take the freedom of expression and the integrity and openness of the overriding educational mission of Yale, through teaching, learning, research, and the dissemination of ideas, with the utmost seriousness. This mission is a sacred trust, and everyone affiliated with this place is a trustee of its grand privileges and obligations.

That is the most positive way I can express the nature and purpose of this place of which you are now an essential part. There is another way as well, and that is to say we do not countenance coercion of another by any means, nor do we or will we tolerate harassment or discrimination of another because of the other person's gender or race or religion or handicap or personal sexual preference or personal beliefs. Scrupulous honesty in academic work and personal dealings, respect for the rights and beliefs of others, civility in one's behavior, are norms here, not goals. We expect openness, decency, and mutual respect in all our dealings as much as we expect disagreement, debate, and the reasoned, forceful give-and-take of ideas. Whether or not that is the family style you are accustomed to, it is the way of life and cherished values of the families you have now joined.

In social life and social relations, I encourage you to make as many new friends as possible because your education will flourish only to the extent to which you meet new people and ideas and because years from now you will look back with the greatest fondness on the people— teachers, other students, coaches, counselors, friends—you came to admire and love here. I also trust you will have fun, because while Yale does not have many of the characteristics of a summer camp, neither is it only a machine for knowledge. Pleasure lives here, too, pleasure in the pursuit of ideas and many other pleasures as well. In the pursuit of happiness, as in the pursuit of ideas, none of us is alone. We must be as mindful of the dignity and the rights of others in social or daily life as we are in curricular or academic life.

In all I have said of family and a state of independence, I urge you to engage the paradox I believe we all come to live, that the individual begins to fulfill his or her potential and power through a deepening awareness of and contact with the differing needs and rights of other people. I am urging you not to resolve that paradox but to use your opportunity for education to fulfill that paradox. It takes work. The human race or America or Yale or you in your relations are not a family because someone says so. The encouragement to individual strivings and the shared guardianship of freedoms does not occur because someone declares that the family lives. Labels do not make life, no matter how assiduously or skillfully applied. It takes work.

As we all have, you too may find difficult moments here as you grapple with how best to fit together individual initiative and community custom, how best to maintain tolerance while pressing disagreement, how to remember that the freedoms you assume must be maintained for everyone else too, or yours disappear. But never fear; the challenges of new family responsibilities will provide you with an exciting and endlessly stimulating adventure. Do not doubt for a moment, my friends, your capacities for living fully the paradox of independence and interdependence. Simply remember that you are here for what we are all here for: to be, in an old Yale phrase, thrown upon the resources of your own minds and then to fulfill the promise of those resources by fashioning the crucial human and intellectual connections beyond you.

The thoughts I have shared with you today may strike you as sober, even solemn. Indeed they are serious matters. I speak to you, however, in the spirit of one who himself truly believes in what I have called an American creed. I also speak as one who truly rejoices at your presence here. So let me close by welcoming you most warmly to our family of freedoms and responsibilities and also to all its pleasures, paradoxical and otherwise.

On Congregations, Their Pleasures and Perils

*T*here is in this ancient place a powerful surge to connectedness, or at least to collectivity. Founded by Congregationalists, Yale has always been marked by an instinct for groups, assemblages, aggregations. The place effortlessly generates congregations, and—while Yale has been, and I trust forever will be, hospitable to the entrepreneur of the mind, the solitary genius, the happy loner— the intellectual and social landscape is dotted with collectivities and sodalities, small bands and teams and caucuses and alliances and societies and committees and gaggles and clutches, their size never fixed but ideally not varying much between a dozen and a dozen and a half, such a span embracing most singing groups, theatrical troupes, publication staffs, much of an entryway, many joint research efforts, senior societies, almost all seminars, a large number of clubs and organizations, and the Yale Corporation.[*]

Delivered to the senior class as the baccalaureate address, May 1986.

[*] The name for the Board of Trustees.

There are smaller aggregations on the campus and larger ones, but Yale since its beginnings has valued amiable affiliation and was fertile ground in the nineteenth century for the growth of a powerful athletic tradition, on the one hand, and the new style of professional or research-oriented groups or schools, on the other, both extensions of its congregating instinct. Whether by way of Walter Camp or Josiah Willard Gibbs, the New England college on its way to becoming a university taught a nation what to expect in sport or in science, in fine arts or law or music or medicine or divinity or letters; it found a formula for concentrating or compounding intellectual and ethical force—keep the place small, keep the internal ties strong, make the communities that form the whole intelligible and manageable. In this way still, the people who are the place find each other and combine in all those patterns that make a dynamic association of minds and spirits. It is not surprising that twentieth-century Yale was capable of gloriously institutionalizing the instinct for affiliation in the College Plan; the residential colleges gave the older impulse to congregate a specific set of shapes and boundaries. It is not surprising that the impetus for the College Plan, where living and learning occur together and friendship is the foundation for education, came from one who had been, as a student in nineteenth-century Yale College, a lonely listener at the lively table talk of Yale. William L. Harkness wanted no one who looked for companionship of the heart and mind, as he had, to be without the opportunity, amid the hustle and bustle, to find the group or circle, the touch of family, that he had missed.

Old Congregationalism, now secular in ways unthinkable at the beginning but still recognizable in its democratic, self-reliant breadth, lives in the College and therefore the University. There can be, as there always have been, however, profound perils in this fidelity to the ideal of small, overlapping communities. Parochialism rather than mutuality can result; cliques rather than community can evolve; smugness—as we happy few glory in each other—can and does occur. And worse than smugness, there occurs at times a tyranny of group self-righteousness, manifesting itself in a rage to ideological or dogmatic purity, a sense that if you are not as devoted to my beliefs as I am, you cannot share this pure ether with me; if you do not replicate my experience and share my goals, you are not let in— there is no room in the group for anyone who does not subscribe to The Doctrine, whatever it may be. That strain of intolerance, of self-righteous self-regard, also derives from the character of Yale's founders and also informs the instinct to aggregate and affiliate, though in a spirit of exclusion, not inclusion; in a spirit of strict party discipline, not like-minded respect. The old Puritans were convinced they knew what Truth was; theirs was a moral absolutism imbued with a pure, inner light. At our origins, there was an absolutism that was itself a form of energy— mindless because it had transcended rational categories, convinced of its own purity and indifferent to dialogue or differentness. And that strain, too, lives on.

I come to these ruminations on the nature and character of our place after nearly thirty years here. As I think back and look forward, I see how nothing is straightforward, nothing is unambiguous; nothing I can see is without risk, is unmixed. Salvation does not come through simplicities, either of sentiment or of system. The gray, grainy, complex nature of existence and the ragged edges of our lives as we actually lead them defy hunger for a neat, bordered existence and for spirits unsullied by doubt or despair. The very instinct for community that marks Yale at its best, the capacity to create those polities that connect lives and minds, is an ideal to be cherished and, as I have thought about it, an impulse to be regarded with skepticism.

This simply means that love and hate are fed, as Blake said, by the same nerve, that the force that includes can also definitively exclude, that the desire for something more perfect can, in its very intensity, deny the freedom it would affirm. It means that truth is perhaps precisely a dynamic compound of opposites, savage contraries for a moment conjoined, and not a single or a simple or a sentimental fixed point. It means that the provisional alone is lasting. Finally, it means that while one must have courage, and a sense of moral direction, it must be the courage of one's own convictions, not someone else's, and the moral direction must be guided by the compass you have set, steering by the compound of all your contradictory inner truths— the visceral, the openhearted, the tough-minded.

I also mean something else: that the health of education, or of educational institutions, rests on the need constantly to be mindful of the crucial distinction between education and indoctrination. While such a distinction may seem obvious, it is not in my experience obvious to everyone. There are many who lust for the simple answers of doctrine or decree. They are on the Left and the Right. They are not confined to a single part of the society. They are terrorists of the mind.

Doctrine closes the mind and kills the spirit, rather than leads to freedom, whenever a doctrine is construed as self-contained and closed, whenever it requires exclusivity of adherence or application or both, and whenever it claims to explain all that has happened to humanity or will happen. Then there is only what I referred to before as a rage to purity, purity in any doctrine so conceived always meaning initially complete submission to the truth as propounded by the true believers. This condition obtained in Nazi Germany with the most systematically evil results; it has obtained elsewhere, including at present in the Soviet empire, in parts of Asia, in parts of Latin America and the Middle East, and, through the evil system of apartheid, in South Africa. Systematic, state-sponsored denial of freedom for some or all is enforced by brute strength and might of arms.

It is at bottom, however, sustained by the systematic and enforced propagation of a closed set of beliefs as if there were no legitimacy to any other view of any kind. Such indoctrination, and the capacity of human beings to submit to, or at times to embrace, the closure and specious completeness of state-enforced indoctrination, is what we must always and ever beware. The best way over time and in time to combat indoctrination by any system that would exclude or master others is to create and foster a principle and process of education that is emphatically not doctrinal or intent on indoctrination. Such an education, of the kind you have been offered and have given yourselves here, will constantly test rather than impose the values it cherishes and will posit seeking truth rather than propounding the truth as its goal. Such an education is finally a lifelong process, not the forced absorption of a static, closed system of belief, and its purpose is to free the mind rather than enclose it.

At the heart of such an education—you know what it is called here; it is called a liberal education—lives the conviction, derived from the Greeks, that freedom of thought is the necessary precondition to political freedom. If freedom, with all its freely chosen constraints, does not first reside in the mind, it cannot finally reside anywhere. Such an education, with a sense of history at its core, does not magically confer freedom of mind and spirit. Rather, by the pursuit of learning for its own sake, by the pursuit of truth wherever it may lie, by the pursuit of those limits that must be learned in order to be surpassed— by these pursuits the mind and spirit are exercised. The mind and spirit are toughened and made capacious in the habits and conditions of freedom, a freedom based on an order, giving of itself so that others may pursue the same compound of boundary and boundlessness, restraint and release, an order earned for freedom's sake. Such an education offers the noblest means by which freedom may be defined for our children, and by them.

The work is never complete, nor may one desist from it. In that thought, drawn from a saying of Rabbi Tarphon, there is a note characteristic of Yale at its beginning and now. For the joy of making with the mind and the work of making with the mind go together. The compound of joy and work is yet another mysterious and compelling form of energy from the old Puritans, transmitted to us as well through the instinct to aggregate in order to educate, to congregate for learning so that life will be bearable.

We are back where we began, back to Yale's changing yet continuous insistence that its people know the good so that they will do it. How deeply this place wants to do what is right, how deeply it wants individuals to determine each for each what the good is. The ability to generate and sanction small groups, with all the risks of parochial self-righteousness that small groups carry with them, is Yale's solution to the problem of how best to mediate between an institutional set of certitudes and an individual's need to exercise choice. Whatever the reasons Yale has chosen to foster certain internal forms of autonomy and affiliation, they have been conceived neither as complete and closed nor as free-floating, innocent of history and obligations. Every center of learning chooses in time how to provide its inhabitants with arenas for making choices. This one has, over time, believed it is important that as individuals or as aggregations, we defend our rights, privileges, and responsibilities, but that each of us also learns that he or she is not alone, that other individuals and congregations have the same rights, the same responsibilities, perhaps a similar instinct to make the shape of something better.

So in its never perfect fashion has Yale continuously returned to America and the world women and men who have learned to care for more than simply themselves. After thirty years, that is what I have come, after all due skepticism, to love in our Yale, the abiding belief in the value and virtue of affiliation. For all its potential and sometimes actual parochialism, I have come to admire the endless energy that flows from here in the service of connection, connection of ideas, of values, of spirit, of people, connection whose compound is that shared sense of life we call civilization.

»» Power, Politics, and a Sense of History »«

One of our most sensible commentators on education and society recently published a brief piece that was deeply disturbing for what it said, yet again, about America's confusion about ideas and power and the power of ideas in our national life. Briefly, this commentator, dismayed because Professor James Coleman had written a report holding "that private high schools seemed to provide a better education than public ones," went to considerable lengths to chide social scientists for having or wishing to have an impact on the course and conduct of national life. Thinking about society is splendid, he seemed to say, as long as the thinkers remain uninvolved in public policy and its creation. "Sociology gains in prestige and value when it keeps its distance from the political battles of the day."*

Delivered to the senior class as the baccalaureate address, May 1981.

* *New York Times,* May 11, 1981, Editorial Notebook.

Presumably, politicians, who fight the battles of the day, fight them better when they do not have the benefit of thinking. Why thoughtful people have chosen to join the gang on the crowded anti–social science bandwagon is a question I cannot answer. Most disturbing to me is the statement "If those who wield political power are to make use of sociological studies—and they should—the research should be neutral both in fact and appearance." I believe our commentator wants research that is nonpartisan, as do I. If he wants, however, social science research that is encouraged to believe itself free of values and disconnected from the world it studies, then he wants soulless, "academic" theorizing that will be of no use to anyone.

To wish a world where ideas are "value free," freeze-dried commodities, and where political power is necessarily unconnected with reflection or analysis about society, is to wish for more of what we have at a time when we need much less of it. Our problem as a society is that we have fostered disconnectedness; we have created a false separateness between social research and policy-making, thinking and politics, ideas and power. At some point, we became unmoored from that fundamental Western concept of a society where the leader and the system he energizes were meant to blend thought and action, ideas with force and forceful ethical behavior. Read Plato's *Statesman,* where the leader fosters education and education furthers the weaving of the web of the state, meshing as in a tapestry the various types of citizens; read Cicero's *Republic,* where the state is a harmonious orchestra, blending like musical tones the various classes, a concord aided by an idea of justice; read these, and whatever you think of them, you will not find a vision of a state where ideas and power can be distinct, where the power of ideas could ever be unconnected to a forceful public good.

For those whose education has been for the purpose of directing ideas to a life of leadership and service to others, whose education has been to see and feel and think about the connectedness among things and how that connectedness must be fostered so that civilization is sustained, my theme is power and a sense of history in our public life. What concerns me most is the way we have disconnected ideas from power in America and created for ourselves thoughtful citizens who disdain politics and politicians, when more than ever we need to value politics and what politicians do; when more than ever we need to recognize that the calling to public life is one of the highest callings a society can make. We need to recognize that if we do not summon and send forth from ourselves a few of the highest quality to lead, the many cannot hold together in civility and dignity.

If a society assumes its politicians are venal, stupid, or self-serving, it will attract to its public life as an ongoing self-fulfilling prophecy the greedy, the knavish, and the dim. If, as I will argue later, a culture like ours has wrongly persuaded itself that power is really mere force, and the use of power in its public or private life simply the exercise of force, then that culture will attract to leadership those who misunderstand power and who therefore cannot possibly use it correctly or well. How power is conceived in a society has the most to do with determining who is attracted to positions of power. A healthy society must never wish to have as its public servants people who hunger only to be in public life, who, thinking power is a natural force, believe they will become immortal if they can tap into its sheer, natural flow. The best way to avoid such people is to avoid such an idea of power.

Far better to think historically, to remember the lessons of the past. Thus, far better to conceive of power as consisting in part of the knowledge of when not to use all the power you have. Far better to be one who knows that if you reserve the power not to use all your power, you will lead others far more successfully and well, for to restrain power is in effect to share it. To share power is to give power to those who do not have it. Whoever knows how to restrain and effectively release power finds, if he is skillful and good, that power flows back to him. Power flows back to such a leader because from the sharing of power comes stability in a society, and stability is finally what humankind aches for, a stability that is just and equitable and humane. On the other hand, those who think of power as simple force to be unleashed, force of personality, force of followers, force of might, force with no historical roots and no sense of consequence, invariably find that they exhaust their power, or are exhausted by it; they find that they only call forth their opposites and that then society inevitably swings, sickeningly, back and forth among those thoughtless enough to consume power because they will not share, and thus replenish, it. Under such leaders, the body politic suffers seizures but never achieves stability. No one wins.

This layman's view of how power in a democracy ought to be construed depends for its efficacy upon those who are attracted to public life; it requires those who are impelled by talent for connectedness rather than by ambition for aggrandized private pleasure; its efficacy depends upon politicians who view the act of governing not as the exercise of sheer pressure but as the assertion of compelling principle. I believe that we have a number of such people serving at the local and the national levels, and that we do not appreciate them as we should. I also believe we ought to be concerned by the spectacle of so many experienced and able elected officials, at all levels, retiring from public service because they will no longer put up with the casual unappreciation by the very people who elected them or with the gnawing of special-interest groups or with the constant high whine emitted by the herds of lobbyists. Finally, we must recognize that we have been so disdainful of or inattentive to our political system that it is increasingly difficult to find candidates who assume the need for any measure of professionalism as a prerequisite for public service.

By professionalism in politics I mean that one should serve an apprenticeship in how to serve, that women and men be encouraged and trained in how to be responsive in a democracy as well as responsible for democratic values. Increasingly we elect, on the basis of powerful advertising campaigns, people who do not know how to do anything for anybody, whether it is having a streetlight installed or protecting a citizen against loss of liberty. Increasingly we elect people who are governed by their staffs, whom no one elected. By professionalism, I mean we must find people who know how and when to subordinate personal obsession to the wishes or will of those they represent, wishes or will those politicians comprehend by returning to where they came from to talk to the people, not by counting editorials or by reading polls. People with professionalism believe politics is an ancient art, not a necessary trial in the world for secular saints or a new game to be played after the rigors of making money are over. Professionalism in public life would never assume that you educate the citizenry to its needs by asserting over and over again that government is best done by dismantling the structures and purposes of government.

While it pleases some to repeat that politics is the art of the possible, I prefer to think that politicians must have the capacity for the impossible—for knowing in which direction their moral compass points and for being supple enough to persuade others of the moral rightness of the course they have set. They must be those who have a clear sense of how complex life is and be willing to make choices they can then convince other thinking people are the correct ones. We are afflicted now, and have been for some time, with solo operators for whom nothing is complex, because nothing is connected to anything else; who believe that the function of government is to impose moralistic schemes rather than to forge complex consensuses, and who treat government as an impediment to mandating purity rather than as a means of connecting, and negotiating among, legitimate needs and achieving a practical, equitable balance. I am disheartened that for at least a decade we have been told by our shepherds that government or the other shepherds are the "enemy." Government is not the enemy, and neither are the people who elect governments. If we elect those who play on the forces that divide us, who play to our fears, we court a tragedy we may not be able to contain. And if we continue to elect those who denigrate what they pursue, who insist they are outsiders as they claw their way to the inside, we ought to ask if it is in our common interest to buy any more snake oil.

Where did it all start in our culture, this worship of power as force, this contempt for restraining or complex connections, and the consequent devaluation of political life? I am not really sure, but I choose to speculate it began in the middle of the last century, as America was collapsing into and struggling out of the ruins of the Civil War. I think it began with those who were best positioned to bypass the founders and to summon up the original strength of Puritan America and to hurl that strength, naked, squalling as if newborn, into the gathering darkness. I believe it began with prophets of the secular religion that was the new America, like Emerson. In 1860, Emerson published his essay "Power" in *The Conduct of Life*.

In the dark pages of that powerful meditation on power, on the eve of the war, Emerson amply reflects a view of politics and politicians that is disdainful of the hurly-burly, the compromising, and the dirtiness of it all. But Emerson makes it clear that he does not share those fastidious views. Those views, he says, are held only by the "timid man"; by the "churchmen and men of refinement," implicitly effete and bookish. Emerson was not for them. He was for the man who is strong, healthy, unfettered, the man who knows that nothing is got for nothing and who will stop at nothing to put himself in touch with events and their force. He is willing to say, because he believes it, "Society is a troop of thinkers, and the best heads among them take the best places," but the metaphor of the mounted squadron, with the best jostling to the fore, means that this is a special kind of thinker. He is, as the immediately preceding sentence says, one who knows "[t]here is always room for a man of force, and he makes room for many." The "thinkers" Emerson really admires are those with "coarse energy,—the 'bruisers,' who have run the gauntlet of caucus and tavern through the county or the state,—" the politicians who despite their vices have "the good-nature of strength and courage." And what do the political bruisers know? They know what Emerson knows:

> the key to all ages is—Imbecility; imbecility in the vast majority of men at all times, and even in heroes in all but certain eminent moments; victims of gravity, custom, and fear. This gives force to the strong,—that the multitude have no habit of self-reliance or original action.

With extraordinary literary skills at a crucial moment in our nation's life, it is Emerson who freed our politics and our politicians from any sense of restraint by extolling self-generated, unaffiliated power as the best foot to place in the small of the back of the man in front of you, and who promoted shoving as the highest calling that abolitionist, moral New England could conceive.

Emerson was a potent figure in his time, and his influence in our culture is powerful to this day. You do not have to read the prophet to realize that his ideas are all around us. Strangely enough, he lives in the popular imagination as the Lover of Nature, a sweet, sentimental, Yankee Kahlil Gibran. In fact, Emerson is as sweet as barbed wire, and his sentimentality as accommodating as a brick. There might have been no lasting harm in all this, no lasting harm in his hymns to the strong and to a strength deriving from a frenzied harmony with the higher laws of Nature; no great harm, though enough, from his wishing for a politics where energy, will and ferocious concentration were the royal roads to success; no real danger from his worship of "self-reliance and original action," except that, like all implacable saviors, Emerson knew where his people were most insecure and where he could best make his balm as indispensable as blood. His everlasting harm comes because he knew Americans would forever feel themselves colonists and thus forever feel themselves derived, or secondhand. And so his greatest contribution to our culture, and greatest disservice, lies in the assurances with which in subtle and obvious ways he justified the jettisoning of history.

Emerson found in our independent character xenophobia, and he made it into a gospel. He managed to persuade generations that custom was a crutch, not a means of continuity; he assured everyman that he was his own pure source and that every native strain in his character was a link with Higher Nature. He wished to sever America from Europe, and American culture and scholarship and politics from whatever humankind had fashioned before. And he thought he had done something good.

The result is that he infected American culture with a scorn of the past. The result is he encouraged America to shake loose from any constraint on our strength and then to call the resulting power miraculous because it had no moorings. Thus, to Emerson I believe we owe our worship of a politics that wishes for originality in all things: for a society in its origins pure, for solutions that are wondrously complete, for politicians whose sheer unthinking vigor will cleanse us forever. To Emerson we owe that spirit of Puritan America that has survived to today, the smug, abstract moralism that is distrustful of any accommodation, that is always certain of its righteousness because it is merely self-regarding, that is scornful of any flexibility of spirit because it has never looked over its shoulder. Emerson and those who followed him licensed that unstable strain in us that would have us begin all over again every morning, every morning to discover evil again in order every morning to focus the will in order to shove our way to noontime; that naive energy that legitimizes those gusts of moralistic frenzy masquerading as high principle that periodically seize us by the throat and that, while always comfortable with nostalgia, are never truly attentive to history. Emerson licensed our violent swings from extreme to extreme by insisting that whatever willful impulse sits in the throne of the heart holds legitimate sway. In another creed, his self-reliance would be the sin of pride.

Rootless save for immersion in the rich soil of the endlessly admiring self, glowing with animal energy, completely devoid of any sense of our common past, a new technocrat of force, Emerson's figure of power formed more than the nineteenth and much of the twentieth centuries' view of the politician. It formed what became an acceptable public personality, and that view of power and its uses is still with us; and it still calls forth reactions to itself as extreme as it is. That is why I lay at Emerson's cottage door the encouragement to instability that is one of America's real afflictions.

Emerson's views are those of a brazen adolescent, and we ought to be rid of them. The maturing of America will occur when we have absorbed, not rejected, our past, our past as various peoples from diverse cultures, not simply as entrepreneurs of the soul. We will mature fully when we require a sense of history in those who lead us, and reject those originals who believe, in whatever walk of life, that each of us is created afresh solely for the purpose of baying at every new, pure moon. The maturing of our politics, which is to say the fashioning of our national life as a work of art, will come when stability of society, not originality of action, is our goal.

To assume that civility—and not success in forcing new purities—is the proper end of politics is to begin to rid this country of the extraordinary savagery of spirit that is now abroad: the resentment at the advancement of others, the bitterness that begrudges everyone else everything, the increasing and deeply dangerous polarization of the races, the pustular eruptions of sexism, racism, and of anti-Semitism whose stench now fills the air. These are all signs that some now feel licensed to shove again the less numerous, the weaker, the new, the exotic, the foreign. I smell that spirit in the air and read it in the papers, I see it in the mail I get, I read it spray-painted on walls, I hear it in the jokes people tell, and it is imperative that all of us condemn and exorcise that spirit. We must civilly, but absolutely clearly reject a spirit that instinctively turns to boycott, instead of tough, reasoned debate, to express its disagreement. We must publicly reject the movement that once again cries to ban books in libraries. We must insist on law, not on rule by decree; we must insist that the principles of the Constitution be applied through the courts and resist the desire that the Constitution be endlessly amended. We must never lose sight of the need for a balanced, pluralistic society, where ideas compete and principles are adjudged by legislative processes and judicial forums. If the day is won by the neo-Puritans through those means, so be it. But those who simply, arrogantly assert that their morality is in the majority should not expect others who simply do not believe it to stand mute.

A civil society can be shattered by the kind of coercion that now seeks to become commonplace.

These tensions and many others are the stuff of our local and national public life, and must be managed by our politicians and by the rest of us. We should honor those who are willing to confront them, and we must insist that they and we do not acquiesce in their divisive force. We must encourage a regard for those who manage our public needs and desires, and if we do not find that regard justified, then we must find and encourage those in whom we can believe and who are worthy of our trust. We must insist that the goal of our politics is not punishment of some group or tendency but healing, a healing of the wounds that the world will always inflict on us all; we must remember and insist that our leaders know that exclusion was never the purpose of our country's dream. We must remember that America was not founded to create exiles.

America's founders intended that we manage, by an act of the will, competing as well as complementary freedoms, in the interests of forging a civil state and a free, generous people. That is not impossibly high idealism, and we cannot let our public life fall to disconnected fragments by scorning its call, or by ignoring its imperatives. High idealism is America's most practical and durable product, our best native handicraft. Those who founded this Republic knew that, and it is the obligation of our political leaders and of the rest of us who elect them to remember it too. It is our obligation to remember that the promise of our history lives in each of us as a sacred trust. What a grand and precious gift, that legacy of competing freedoms all urging us to liberality of spirit and a decent public order.

Part Two

THE EARTHLY
USE OF A LIBERAL
EDUCATION

⫸ A Liberal Education and the New Coercion ⫷

*H*ere at Yale you will hear often about a liberal education. What is it? Is a liberal education a set of courses, fulfilling certain requirements, across a variety of disciplines? That is certainly a description of the mechanics of what might become a liberal education. Is it an education pursued, as Cardinal Newman believed, in a spirit that studies a subject simply for and in itself, without concern for the practical consequences of such study? That would be the description of the proper attitude to bring to your studies. There is, however, more to what I mean by a liberal education.

I believe a liberal education is an education in the root meaning of *liberal—liber,* "free"—the liberty of the mind free to explore itself, to draw itself out, to connect with other minds and spirits in the quest for truth. Its goal is to train the whole person to be at once intellectually discern-

Freshman address, August 1981.

ing and humanly flexible, tough-minded and openhearted; to be responsive to the new and responsible for values that make us civilized. It is to teach us to meet what is new and different with reasoned judgment and humanity. A liberal education is an education for freedom, the freedom to assert the liberty of the mind to make itself new for the other minds it cherishes.

The order necessary to keep that freedom from collapsing into merely competitive appetites or colliding gusts of anarchy is, first, in this country, a respect for law and the processes of law. But it is also more than an order external; it is the internalized order that grows with self-government, self-civilizing. Order is the precondition of humane freedom, freedom the goal of responsible order. Your education here intends to do many things, but ultimately it intends to bring you to comprehend the responsibilities and the pleasures of that essential, grand connection.

I speak to the nature of a liberal education, and of freedom and order, for three reasons. First, I believe it cannot be said often enough how precious and vital these ideas are to our daily lives. Second, I raise them because the practical application of these principles will be, I hope, the defining framework for your time at Yale and for your lives after Yale. And, third, I raise them because I think they must be asserted at this particular time in our country's history, in the teeth of a storm that blows across the landscape. I have said what I believe because there are now in America powerful voices that attack and will continue to attack these very ideas.

A self-proclaimed "Moral Majority," and its satellite or client groups, cunning in the use of a native blend of old intimidation and new technology, threatens the values

I have named. Angry at change, rigid in the application of chauvinistic slogans, absolutistic in morality, its members threaten through political pressure or public denunciation whoever dares to disagree with their authoritarian positions. Using television, direct mail, and economic boycott, they would sweep before them anyone who holds a different opinion.

From the maw of this "morality" come those who presume to know what justice for all is; come those who presume to know which books are fit to read, which television programs are fit to watch, which textbooks will serve for all the young; come spilling those who presume to know what God alone knows, which is when human life begins. From the maw of this "morality" rise the tax-exempt Savanarolas who believe they, and they alone, possess the truth. There is no debate, no discussion, no dissent. They know. There is only one set of overarching political and spiritual and social beliefs; whatever view does not conform to these views is by definition relativistic, negative, secular, immoral, against the family, anti–free enterprise, un-American. What nonsense.

What dangerous, malicious nonsense. What a shame more of our captains of commerce have not seized the opportunity to speak up *for* free enterprise. What a shame such denials of our country's deepest traditions of freedom of thought, speech, creed, and choice are not faced candidly in open debate by our political and religious leaders. What a shame more of those from various parts of the society with the responsibility to lead have not made the point, clearly and unambiguously, that such beliefs have every right to be expressed but not to be imposed by intimidation.

I do not fear that these peddlers of coercion will eventually triumph. The American people are too decent, too generous, too practical about their principles, to put up with the absolutism of these "majorities" for very long. Nor do I think that when these groups have finally gone back into their burrows of frustration and anger, to lie seething until the next time, the values they now pervert will be done lasting harm. For what they claim they espouse—love of country, a regard for the sanctity of life and the importance of the family, a belief in high standards of personal conduct, a conviction that we derive our values from a transcendent being, a desire to assert that free enterprise is better than state ownership or state control—are not evil or pernicious beliefs. Quite the contrary. They are the kernels of beliefs held dear, in various ways, by me and by millions of other Americans. You should not scorn these ideas simply because some extremists claim, whether sincerely or hypocritically, to have captured these beliefs for themselves. The point is, the rest of us hold to ideas of family, country, belief in God, *in different ways*. The right to differ, and to see things differently, is our concern.

What disgusts me so much about the "morality" seeping out of the ground around our feet is that it would deny the legitimacy of differentness. We should all be dismayed with the shredding of the spiritual fabric of our society, with the urging to selfishness and discrimination all around us. We should be concerned that so much of our political and religious leadership acts intimidated for the moment and will not say with clarity that this most recent denial of the legitimacy of difference is a radical assault on the very pluralism—of peoples, political beliefs, values, forms of merit, and systems of religion—our country was founded to welcome and foster.

Pluralism is not relativism. It does not mean the denial of absolutes or the absence of standards. Pluralism is not code for anything. It signals the recognition that people of different ethnic groups and races and adherents of various religious and political and personal beliefs have a right to coexist as equals under the law and have an obligation to forge the freedoms they enjoy into a coherent, civilized, and vigilant whole. These different peoples have a responsibility, inherent in their freedom, to make a commonweal, that is, a public good whose abiding concern is the practical protection of the several individual freedoms that are ordered for the general welfare. If pluralism as a concept denies anything, it denies the hegemony of the homogeneous, the rule by a single, overmastering sensibility that would exclude from the general benefits of citizenship all those who are different.

Pluralism is an inclusive, absorptive ideal; in practical terms, it encourages competition, compromise, and consensus. It does not abide absolutism, decree, and complete moral certitude. In political terms, a pluralistic democracy like ours is often messy; issues are not neat, edges are not clean, resolution is not swift in most cases, because so many different interests must be attended to. One can lament the special- or single-interest lobby; one can grow mightily impatient with a Congress, for instance, that always trades off and spreads the pain or the pork on a national basis. Nor is a pluralistic democracy any more immune to corruption than are other aggregations of humankind. For the governors and the governed, the consensual, complex, compromising mode of a democracy can be wearing and wearying. But how much better a system that does not assume that one single voice shall forever have the last say; how much better a shifting, adaptive if imperfect public process, concerned finally to keep its questions open and essential freedoms strong, than one that would displace law with video mysticism and would presume to impose a final, complete, arbitrary contour on society and the behavior of individuals. The Moral Majority is a cry of exhaustion, a longing for surcease from the strain of managing complexity.

Those voices of coercion speak not for liberty but for license, the license to divide in the name of patriotism, the license to deny in the name of Christianity. And they have licensed a new meanness of spirit in our land, a resurgent bigotry that manifests itself in racist and discriminatory postures, in threats of political retaliation, in injunctions to censorship, in acts of violence.

In December of 1980, the Anti-Defamation League of B'nai B'rith stated that reported anti-Semitic episodes, including vandalism, arson, and cemetery desecrations, increased by 192 percent in 1980—from 129 episodes in 1979 to 377 in 1980. The tip of the iceberg grew in a way that sickened all decent Americans. In the past few years, the Ku Klux Klan has increased its visibility again and claims to have founded or revived, in its name or in league with others, paramilitary camps and training activities in Alabama, California, Connecticut, Illinois, North Carolina, and Texas.

Hating in public by the mad or the malevolent is only part of the story being told again. People who have no connection or sympathy with such forms of domestic terrorism nevertheless use the new atmosphere to apologize for other forms of terrorism; or they fall silent when it is imperative precisely to speak out; or they apologize for the excesses—the spiritual violence—of evangelical or political fringe groups. In the new atmosphere, it becomes possible to keep, as Jack Newfield among others has said, two sets of books on civil liberties, two sets of standards that can be applied as one's ideology demands, rather than the single standard set forth by the Bill of Rights, the "monism" of values, that a pluralistic society must maintain to be healthy, open, and free. It is a new mood that can be quantified only up to a point, a mood that should not be dismissed as either inevitable—the consequence of a national "swing to the right"—or as historically predictable—the cyclic eruptions of Know-Nothingism or a recurrent "paranoid style" in American life. Neither of those "explanations" serves, because each avoids the issue. The issue is that a reactionary mood, preying on the fears of those who feel dispossessed by change and bypassed by complexity, is growing and that there is a moral imperative, rooted in America's best traditions, to identify it and call for a cleansing of the air.

The people who make these efforts to deny others the freedom to be themselves wish for a closed society, a form of community similar to a vast, airless bunker. That is not the kind of community you have come to and that has been waiting to welcome you. Yale is a diverse, open place, receptive to people from throughout our society, and it must and will remain so. It is a University community given to the competition of ideas and of merit, devoted to excellence, and dedicated to the belief that freedom of choice, speech, and creed is essential to the quest for truth that constitutes its mission. Those who wish such a place to teach only their version of the "right" values and "correct" views misunderstand completely the free market of ideas that is a great university; they misapprehend the extent to which the University serves the country best when it is a caldron of competing ideas and not a neatly arranged platter of received opinions.

You will find, if Yale is at all successful, much that is different here. Revel in that diversity. Whether different idea or person, connect with it in order to understand it. Female and male, Christian and Jew, black, white, brown, and yellow, you must find, as we all must, what binds us together, in common hope and need, not what divides us. You may or may not all come to love one another, but to be part of the best of this place you must have the moral courage to respect one another. This is not a community that will tolerate the sexism, the racism, the anti-Semitism, the bigotry about ethnic groups, the hysterical rejection of others, the closing off and closing in, that is now in the air. The spirit that sends hate mail, paints swastikas on walls, burns crosses, bans books—vandalizes minds—has no place here. We must, and we will, maintain at Yale a spirit that is tolerant, respectful, and candid, for that spirit is the form of order essential to sustain the freedom of the mind inquiring.

Such a spirit in the service of the inquiring mind is the responsibility of everyone in this community—students, faculty, staff, alumni, all those affiliated with Yale in any way. We can all fulfill our purposes in this institution of learning only when we face that responsibility, and what it means, with zest and dignity. We must, therefore, civilly and clearly have the courage to reject bigotry and coercion in all forms and have the courage to embrace the intellectual and human diversity of our community and our country. We cannot as Americans succumb to the fatigue, the arrogance mixed with exhaustion, that claims an exclusive "morality" and that negates and denies. To do so would be to betray at the deepest levels what a free people have won, through struggle and pain, over three centuries.

⪢ *The Earthly Use of a Liberal Education* ⪡

The summer before college is the time when in a thousand different circumstances mythology dresses up as epistemology. Parents, older siblings and friends, former teachers, coaches, and employers, dimly but vividly remembering how it was, propound with certainty how they know the way it might, or should, or could, or will be.

By and large, the versions of your life to come are well meant. All summer long, however, you have simply wanted to get on with it. There, of course, is the rub. Despite all you have heard and read, no one can tell you what it is you are now so desirous of getting on with. Nor can anyone tell you what it, whatever it is, will be like. You wonder, Will everyone else know? Will he or she be more sure, less insecure, less new? Will I ever get to know anyone? Will I be able to do it? Whatever it is.

Freshman address, September 1983.

I will tell you, in a moment, what I think it is. I cannot tell you with certainty what it will be like; no one can. Each of us experiences college differently. I can assure you that soon your normal anxieties will recede and a genuine excitement will begin, a rousing motion of the spirit unlike anything you have experienced before. And that will mark the beginning of it, the grand adventure that you now undertake, never alone but on your own, the voyage of exploration in freedom that is the development of your own mind. Generations have preceded you in this splendid opening out of the self as you use the mind to explore the mind, and, if the human race is rational, generations will come after you. But each of you will experience your education uniquely—charting and ordering and dwelling in the land of your own intellect and sensibility, discovering powers you had only dreamed of and mysteries you had not imagined and reaches you had not thought that thought could reach. There will be pain and some considerable loneliness at times, and not all the terrain will be green and refreshing. There will be awesome wastes and depths as well as heights. The adventure of discovery is, however, thrilling because you will sharpen and focus your powers of analysis, of creativity, of rationality, of feeling—of thinking with your whole being. If at Yale you can experience the joy that the acquisition and creation of knowledge for its own sake brings, the adventure will last your whole life and you will have discovered the distinction between living as a full human being and merely existing.

If there is a single term to describe the education that can spark a lifelong love of learning, it is the term *liberal education*. A liberal education has nothing to do with those political designer labels *liberal* and *conservative* that some so lovingly stitch on to every idea they pull off, or put on, the rack. A liberal education is not one that seeks to implant the precepts of a specific religious or political orthodoxy. Nor is it an education intending to prepare for immediate immersion in a profession. That kind of professional education is pursued at Yale at the graduate level in eleven graduate and professional schools. Such training ought to have in it a liberal temper; that is, technical or professional study ought to be animated by a love of learning, but such training is necessarily and properly pointed to the demands and proficiency requirements of a career or profession. Such is not the tendency of an education, or of the educational process, in Yale College.

In Yale College, education is "liberal" in Cardinal Newman's sense of the word. As he says in the fifth discourse of *The Idea of the University,*

> . . . that alone is liberal knowledge which stands on its own pretensions, which is independent of sequel, expects no complement, refuses to be *informed* (as it is called) by any end, or absorbed in any art, in order duly to present itself to our contemplation. The most ordinary pursuits have this specific character, if they are self-sufficient and complete; the highest lose it, when they minister to something beyond them.

As Newman emphasizes, a liberal education is not defined by the content or by the subject matter of a course of study. It is a common error, for instance, to equate a liberal education with the so-called liberal arts or *studia humanitatis.** To study the liberal arts or the humanities

---

* See "A City of Green Thoughts."

is not necessarily to acquire a liberal education unless one studies these and allied subjects in a spirit that, as Newman has it, seeks no immediate sequel, that is independent of a profession's advantage. If you pursue the study of anything not for the intrinsic rewards of exercising and developing the power of the mind but because you press toward a professional goal, then you are pursuing not a liberal education but rather something else.

A liberal education is defined by the attitude of the mind toward the knowledge the mind explores and creates. Such education occurs when you pursue knowledge because you are motivated to experience and absorb what comes of thinking—thinking about the traditions of our common human heritage in all its forms, thinking about new patterns or designs in what the world proffers today—whether in philosophic texts or financial markets or chemical combinations—thinking in order to create new knowledge that others will then explore. A liberal education at Yale College embraces physics as well as French, lasers as well as literature, social science and physical and biological sciences as well as the arts and humanities. A liberal education rests on the supposition that our humanity is enriched by the pursuit of learning for its own sake; it is dedicated to the proposition that growth in thought, and in the power to think, increases the pleasure, breadth, and value of life.

"That is very touching," I will be told, "that is all very well, but how does someone make a living with this joy of learning and pleasure in the pursuit of learning? What is the earthly use of all this kind of education later on, in the practical, real world?" These are not trivial questions, though the presuppositions behind them puzzle me somewhat. I am puzzled, for instance, by the unexamined assumption that the "real world" is always thought to lie outside or beyond the realm of education. I am puzzled by the confident assumption that only in certain parts of daily life do people make "real" decisions and do "real" acts lead to "real" consequences. I am puzzled by those who think that ideas do not have reality or that knowledge is irrelevant to the workings of daily life.

To invert Plato and to believe that ideas are unreal and that their pursuit has no power for practical or useful good is to shrink reality and define ignorance. To speak directly to the questions posed by the skeptic of the idea of a liberal education, I can say only this: ideas and their pursuit define our humanity and make us human. Ideas, embodied in data and values, beliefs, principles, and original insights, must be pursued because they are valuable in themselves and because they are the stuff of life. There is nothing more necessary to the full, free, and decent life of a person or of a people or of the human race than to free the mind by passionately and rationally exercising the mind's power to inquire freely. There can be no more practical education, in my opinion, than one that launches you on the course of fulfilling your human capacities to reason and to imagine freely and that hones your abilities to express the results of your thinking in speech and in writing with logic, clarity, and grace.

While such an education may be deemed impractical by those wedded to the notion that nothing in life is more important than one's career, nevertheless I welcome you to a liberal education's rigorous and demanding pleasures. Fear not, you will not be impeded from making a living because you have learned to think for yourself and because you take pleasure in the operation of the mind and in the pursuit of new ideas. And you will need to make a living. The world will not provide you with sustenance or employment. You will have to work for it. I am instead speaking of another dimension of your lives, the dimension of your spirit that will last longer than a job, that will outlast a profession, that will represent by the end of your time on earth the sum of your human significance. That is the dimension represented by the mind unfettered, "freely ranging onley within the Zodiack of his owne wit," as the old poet said. There is no greater power a human being can develop for the individual's or for the public's good.

And I believe that the good, for individuals and for communities, is the end to which education must tend. I affirm Newman's vision that a liberal education is one seeking no sequel or complement. I take him to be writing of the motive or tendency of the mind operating initially within the educational process. But I believe there is also a larger tendency or motive, which is animated by the pursuit of ideas for their own sake. I believe that the pleasure in the pursuit of knowledge joins and is finally at one with our general human desire for a life elevated by dignity, decency, and moral progress. That larger hope does not come later; it exists inextricably intertwined with a liberal education. The joy of intellectual pursuit and the pursuit of the good and decent life are no more separable than on a fair spring day the sweet breeze is separable from the sunlight.

In the common pursuit of ideas for themselves and of the larger or common good, the freedom that the individual mind wishes for itself, it also seeks for others. How could it be otherwise? In the pursuit of knowledge leading to the good, you cannot wish for others less than you wish for yourself. Thus, in the pursuit of freedom, the individual finds it necessary to order or to limit the surge to freedom so that others in the community are not denied the very condition each of us seeks. A liberal education desires to foster a freedom of the mind that will also contribute, in its measure, to the freedom of others.

We learn, therefore, that there is no true freedom without order; we learn that there are limits to our freedom, limits we learn to choose freely in order not to undermine what we seek. After all, if there were, on the one hand, no restraints at all, only anarchy of intellect and chaos of community would result. On the other hand, if all were restraint, and release of inquiry and thought were stifled, only a death of the spirit and a denial of any freedom could result. There must be an interplay of restraint and release, of order and freedom, in our individual lives and in our life together. Without such interplay within each of us, there can be no good life for any of us. If there is no striving for the good life for all of us, however, there cannot be a good life for any one of us. We must learn how freedom depends for its existence upon freely chosen (because rationally understood) forms of order.

At Yale College, you will find both the spur for freedom of inquiry and civility's curbing rein. One could, I suppose, locate these conditions in the classroom and in the residential colleges; one could posit that in the classroom the release of the mind is encouraged and in the residential colleges the limits to civil behavior are learned. That view is oversimplified, for in both contexts, as well as on playing fields, in community service, in extracurricular activities, in services of worship, in social events, the interplay of freedom and order obtains. In all these contexts, as in each one of us, the surge of freedom and the restraint that compounds freedom's joy and significance occur all the time.

The ideal of this community is therefore composed of intellectual and ethical portions, the freedom of the mind and the freedom to express the results of the mind's inquiry disciplined by the imperative to respect the rights and responsibilities of others. It is a community open to new ideas, to disagreement, to debate, to criticism, to the clash of opinions and convictions, to solitary investigation, to originality, but it is not tolerant of, and will not tolerate, the denial of the dignity and freedoms of others. It will not tolerate theft of another's intellectual product. It will not tolerate denials of another's freedom of expression. It will not tolerate sexist or racist or other acts or expressions of bigotry based on prejudices about ethnic or religious backgrounds or about personal sexual preference or private philosophic or political beliefs. It will not tolerate these denials, because the freedom we possess to foster free inquiry and the greater good is too precious. What I have stated are matters of moral conviction. They are also matters of University policy. The policies that reflect those convictions are designed to protect an environment where individual rights are respected because responsibilities are shared. They are designed to create a community where freedom exists because order is sustained by the moral courage to affirm the good by all members of the community.

I have told you what I think it is, the "it" I guessed you might be concerned with upon your arrival. It is a quest to become the best in all that is meant by being human. This quest has been going on in this College for a long time, in this old New England city by the water. In 1701 Yale made a promise to itself and a pact with America, to contribute to the increase of scholarship, service, and spiritual enlightenment. You now assume part of the obligation of that promise. And you will be essential to maintaining the faith of that pact. As you deepen in the commitment to ideals and in the excellence I know you possess, this community will continue to shape itself in intellectual and ethical ways that are faithful to our ancient roots and in ways that are ever new.

⋙ A City
of Green
Thoughts ⋘

*T*here is a quickening of the blood, a
sense of pleasurable adventure, every autumn in this place
because once again we all gather together, the new people
and those who have gathered before, to start the formal
process of making-with-the-mind that is called education.
Of course, more than the mind is involved, more than
the formal process is engaged, for education is a matter
involving character as well as intellect, the heart and spirit
as well as the mind, the extracurriculum as well as the
formal course of study; education is something longer,
broader, deeper, than the thirteen weeks of instruction
for eight semesters, just as it is more than the learning
that occurs in classroom, laboratory, and library, just as
it is far more than an accumulation of information and
the acquisition of fact and the compilation of grades. A

Earlier versions were first delivered to the Association of Yale Alumni Assembly XXII, "Humanities at Yale," August 1983, and as the freshman address, August 1985.

transcript, for instance, no more tells the story of an education than a railroad timetable tells the story of a journey.

This journey of education is lifelong; it began in your family and your place of worship and in your earlier schools and in the spaces of your soul that are yours alone, and it should go on long after you have left here. But for all that everything contributes to one's education, at the core of the grand process there is the formal part, the central act of learning, focused on those places of pedagogy where older and younger come together. In those places, they come together for conversation, the acts of turning back and forth, of sharing and shaping that every day, in ways innumerable, make connections, connections in and through ideas as palpable and real as anything you will ever encounter, with other minds, past, present, and future. Here green and growing ideas—by patient tending and work, by their open exchange and clash, by the sheer pressure of untrammeled thought—create over time a conversation that, laden with a passionate commitment to values and reason, becomes civilization. So a process moves an individual to membership in a community; so a thought, begun in the seminary of a single mind, participates in the construction of a citadel of living ideas, of a life organic and yet shaped. So we thus make a city of green thoughts, an ingathering of achievement ennobled by aspiration, of ideals tempered by application, a civilized life lived not alone but in concert. All this is what you engage, as your life is now the life of the University, and the University existence begins to animate yours.

You may find such a goal at this moment simply too abstract, and yet let me assure you that it is not beyond you to know that a life of decency, justice, and dignity for us all should be your goal as a human being; it is not a mere abstraction or irrelevance to urge you to approach, as much as your individual powers allow, such a goal by developing, to the fullest extent you can, the powers of your mind in all their rousing strength and reach for what is noble.

It is certainly within the powers of all of you to understand that this is a community that depends upon people sharing the values of openness, mutual respect, and the freedom of all to express themselves. You should know that coercion in any context is anathema in this academic community. We strive here for a civil existence by rejecting judgments based on race, religion, gender, ethnic background, sexual orientation, political or philosophic belief. We strive for a civil society through the consideration of people on their merit and through the free, open, and frank exchange of ideas.

As you now look forward to what lies just ahead, and to all it can mean, there of course will arise in each of you normal anxiety. Such emotion is natural and healthy. What I wish you to avoid, as you continue your journey, is the desire to try to arrange all of the future now. I want you to hold yourselves ready but not rigid. I urge you to keep an open mind. Indeed, the getting and keeping of an open mind, a mind flexible and tough in its powers, humane in its perspective, rational and imaginative in its operations, is the goal of your education here; it is the way to the green city.

The educational process by which the mind is ordered so that it may be open is called a liberal education: training in how to discern those essential human values that make us free; training in how to express, in speech and writing, our commitment to those values in order to keep us free. It is an education at whose core is the study of history, the history of the struggle of individuals or peoples to create institutions—families, games, churches, schools, legal systems, governments—that will preserve an individual's or a people's freedom.

Such an education looks back at our common Western heritage and is one of the central means whereby that heritage is made continuous and available to the future. I wish today to tell you where the powerful idea and reality of a liberal education came from and why it is so important that we keep fresh and new the ancient tradition such an education embodies. I wish to speak of the humanities and of humanistic study.

To discover what is properly meant by the Humanities, we must examine some other words and concepts. Those words and concepts are *Renaissance, humanism, humanist.* Only by that route can we get back to humanities, or *studia humanitatis,* or liberal studies, *studia liberalia.* At that point, we will have arrived at the conjunction of wisdom and eloquence whose expression is necessary to make us free and keep us free. We will proceed to freedom by way of history.

Renaissance. Giorgio Vasari, in his *Lives of the Great Painters, Sculptors, and Architects,* first published in 1550, used the Italian word *rinascita* to describe the rebirth of the arts in the two centuries preceding him. We do not use the Italian word for rebirth to identify the period between 1350 and 1650. We use the French word *renaissance,* and for a good reason. The period of time from the fourteenth to the seventeenth century was not called the "renaissance" until the nineteenth century when the great French historian Jules Michelet published his massive *History of France*. The seventh volume, which appeared in 1855, was entitled *La Renaissance*.

The Renaissance is to some extent, therefore, an invention of the nineteenth century. So also is humanism. *Humanism* as a term was invented in 1808 by a German educator named Friedrich Niethammer when he defended the teaching of Greek and Latin in secondary school curricula, all in an effort to stave off what he viewed as an increasingly practical and vocational secondary schooling. Although *Renaissance* and its central educational movement for the educated elite, *humanism*, derive as terms from the nineteenth century, they have their roots in that three hundred years between the middle of the fourteenth and the middle of the seventeenth century.

Humanism is derived from the word *umanista* or *humanist*. *Humanist*, in Latin, was student slang in the Italian universities in the late fifteenth and early sixteenth centuries. It was a term, formed by analogy with *jurista* or *artista*, that referred to the professional specialists—the professors, teachers, and students—of the Greek and Latin classics, the *studia humanitatis*. These *studia humanitatis*, or humanities, were grammar, rhetoric, history, poetry, and moral philosophy. Humanists were all those who read, wrote, or emulated the ancients and ancient ethical and cultural wisdom by way of those areas of study. Humanists, therefore, were not only professional teachers and students but also secretaries to rulers or cities, civil servants, writers who instructed others in ancient thought and civic virtue. Thus, the Renaissance had at its educational and cultural heart humanism. *Humanism* is defined either as the study and transmission of ancient letters or as the propagation of civic virtue based on ancient ethics and Christian precept. Humanism was the concern of humanists, which is to say of those who professed, in some form, the *studia humanitatis.*

The *studia humanitatis,* or humanities, came from the Romans. Cicero and Gellius, Roman philosophers and orators, had used the term *studia humanitatis* to translate the Greek word *paideia,* which meant education or culture or those cultural values whose study is education and whose apprehension forms the good citizen. These "good arts," as the ancients called them, were the means whereby, the Renaissance said, wisdom was gained; once gained, it was shaped and refined by rhetoric, the art of speaking and writing well that moved the private perception of the good out of the self and into the public, where virtue was then able, if persuasively presented, to shape the free and civil state.

To conjoin wisdom with eloquence, thence to move humankind to virtue in civic or political terms, was the driving ideal behind the study of the ancients and of the subjects of grammar, rhetoric, history, poetry, and moral philosophy. Humanism, the humanists, the study of the humanities, celebrated active engagement with the world, not contemplative repose. The purpose of study was to improve the political life of the community. It was meant to improve the lot of human beings not simply as the ancients had celebrated such a life but as the Christian faith taught as well.

To study the humanities was not simply to study secular subjects and spiritual values. It was also to learn a *method.* The method employed to study these values was philology, that is, the careful examination of what the ancients and the Latin and Greek fathers, and indeed the Bible, actually said, not what they were said to have said. Philology drives one back constantly to sources, to manuscripts, to the roots of words. Philology is a radical approach, concerned with discovering roots and therefore with uncovering origins, so as better to understand the reality of what was, by the Renaissance, perceived as distant in time and separate in concept.

Let me illustrate some of these assertions by citing one of the most influential treatises on education written in the Renaissance. We would now say that this was a powerful treatise on humanism by a humanist about the humanities. Pietro Paulo Vergerio, of Padua, who wrote this treatise in 1403 or 1404, entitled it simply "On the Noble Customs," and some manuscripts later add "And the Liberal Studies." He dedicated it to the son of the lord of Padua. In his work, Vergerio treats the purpose of education for the young, the subjects, how to study, how to exercise and train for war, how to find recreation. He is, like all wise writers on education, interested in the whole person.

He says that *liberal studies,* his term for the humanities, gives first place to history, next to moral philosophy, and third to eloquence.

> By philosophy we learn the essential truth of things, which by eloquence we so exhibit in orderly adornment as to bring conviction to differing minds. And history provides the light of experience—a cumulative wisdom fit to supplement the force of reason and the persuasion of eloquence. For we allow that soundness of judgment, wisdom of speech, integrity of conduct are the marks of a truly liberal temper.[*]

[*] "The Treatise *De Ingenibus Moribus* by Petrus Paulus Vergerius," in William Harrison Woodward, *Vittorino da Feltre and Other Humanist Educators* (1897; reprint, New York: Columbia Teachers College, 1963), pp. 106–7.

After reviewing other disciplines that are also crucial—grammar, poetry, music, arithmetic—Vergerio gives us the clearest statement we could ask of the place of this study in a life.

> Respecting the general place of liberal studies, we remember that Aristotle would not have them absorb the entire interests of life; for he kept steadily in view the nature of man as a citizen, an active member of the State. For the man who has surrendered himself absolutely to the attractions of Letters or speculative thought follows, perhaps, a self-regarding end and is useless as a citizen or as prince. (Woodward, p. 110)

Study should be lifelong but not life consuming. If the life is consumed in study, the study is not shared; if it is not shared, it cannot be useful to others; if not useful to others, it plays no role in shaping a civil state in which all, the learned and the unlearned, may live a free and decent life. The humanities, in short, were elite culture but not the private property of the elite. If a person kept his learning to himself, he had not gained any wisdom. He was merely informed; he had failed to become educated. The humanists knew better than anyone that the word *education* is derived from the Latin *educere*, "to lead out"; it was the leading out of private wisdom for the greater public good that was the constant end of humanistic study.

If that was the end, was that civic goal assured simply by the studying of the humanities and by the sharing of the fruits of that study? Only if the subjects studied are those designed to make one better will the study of them lead one to betterment, Vergerio would have said:

We call those studies *liberal* which are worthy of a free man; those studies by which we attain and practise virtue and wisdom; that education which calls forth, trains and develops those highest gifts of body and of mind which ennoble men, and which are rightly judged to rank next in dignity to virtue only. (Woodward, p. 102)

If those who are free study the liberal arts, study the *studia humanitatis* that exalt freedom and recall the condition of humankind in freedom, then freedom—intellectual and political—will be maintained. It is no accident that humanism, or the study of the humanities, first flourished and spread from Florence and Venice, which were republics, ruled by powerful families, to be sure, but also ruled by elections of those eligible to vote, ruled above all, for all the machinations, by the ideals of the Roman Republic and Periclean Athens.

The humanists devised an educational program based on ancient studies. They believed that such study was a lifelong activity of a citizen. Political freedom was predicated upon freedom of thought; if freedom does not first reside in the mind, it cannot finally reside anywhere. Freedom of thought was necessarily based on those principles and disciplines that trained and toughened the mind, and thus released it, to apprehend the ideals of a full and free life and to make such ideals active and comprehensible to their fellow citizens. The humanities have their origin and their force in the Renaissance and classical programs of education in liberty of mind for liberty of civic behavior. From the Greeks through the nineteenth century, these studies were humanities because they linked the interpretation of words to the active life of a citizen.

Only lately have notions that the humanities have something to do with humaneness, or humanitarianism, or a human-centered universe, or a rejection of spiritual for secular values, arrived to confuse or even undermine the true power and point of the *studia humanitatis*. The self-regarding and sentimental meanings that in the last one hundred years have attached themselves to the humanities are often precisely the opposite of what those who forged the idea of the humanities had in mind.

Because you share with the rest of us the obligation to preserve and enlarge our common store of freedom, I believe you should place at the center of your college education three efforts: to deepen a sense of history, so you will know who you are as human beings and as Americans; to develop your capacity to think analytically and creatively; and to hone the ability to express your thinking in speech and writing with logic, clarity, and grace. By those ordering acts, you will begin to make your minds free and affirm the order and enlarge the freedom of us all.

At the center of your future and ongoing education, I urge you to place this humanistic emphasis. It will be at once the most valuable education you will give yourself and the most practical. There is nothing more enduring and more necessary for a full and decent life for yourself and for family, community, and country than an education that sets as the end of intellectual development a civic goal, that places as the purpose of making a good mind, the making of a good citizen and a polity of justice and dignity.

You will receive vast quantities of advice—about what to study, what to major in, what to pursue in order to gain a spot in some postgraduate school; you will be told by nervous elders to study accounting because it is the real world, and so forth. Simply remember through it all that a balance sheet is no more real than a molecule or a poem or a ballot. Remember that what is real, and really enduring, starts in acts of the disciplined imagination, acts of insight and definition that create and discover a larger design, and that a mind historically informed, and clear in thought and expression, will make such reality and thus redeem whatever simply is, by making what ought to be. For such a mind, summoning the resources of heart and spirit can create that shared life of aspiration and achievement that we call civilization.

⫸ On Behalf of
the Humanities ⫷

Of all the areas in colleges and universities that will feel the assaults of inflation, the shrinking numbers of students, the devastated job market, and particularly the growing vocationalism of the young, the humanities will be hardest hit. Yet, if one speaks of the values, and value, of a liberal education, the humanities ought to be central to the conversation. My concerns are for the continuing, vital existence of the humanities.

I conceive of the humanities as those areas of inquiry that are language- or, better, word-centered, and I conceive of the radical humanist activity, therefore, as revolving around the interpretation of a text. My logocentricity is part of an old, relatively unphilosophic, fundamentally philological tradition. It sees language as the bearer of tradition, believes words give first principles and last things,

Delivered at a conference on the humanities at Yale in 1977 and then at the convention of the Modern Language Association, New York, December 1978.

and therefore believes that if etymology and eschatology will finally converge to clarify the life of an individual or an institution or a people, it will be because texts and the varieties of interpretation are vital concerns to that individual or institution or people. "*Connexa sunt studia humanitatis,*" said Coluccio Salutati, at the end of the fourteenth century. He was talking about the crucial role of grammar in the divine scheme of things. "Humane studies are connected to each other; religious studies are also bound each to each; it is impossible to acquire a complete knowledge of the one science without the other." If the humanist perspective sees how things secular and sacred are connected among themselves, it sees that connection through the ligatures of language. And it is the tradition of seeing from various vantage points, the principle of perspective and hence of multiple perspectives, that the humanities want to keep alive and well.

That is my bias, which no one is obliged to share or even approve. But it is beneath what follows—which is a sense that in the last decade incoherence has often been institutionalized; that most curricula in high school and beyond are no better structured than many student papers; that where requirements were replaced by guidelines, those guidelines are so lacking in force they could not guide a vulture to week-old carrion, much less anyone to self-education. It is my sense that, in general, we still tend to apply solutions of the 1960s to problems of the 1970s and 1980s—and those solutions do not necessarily work.

The structures and the habits of mind of a period that was expansionist, federally supported and student oriented; of a time when faith in the college or university mission as aimed at social action was at its most intense; of a time when it was easier than ever before to assert that academic work ought to be in many ways a form of social work—the specific attitudes of that period are in some places still being asserted and assumed when those days are gone. Demographic projections now point to a dramatic lessening in numbers of college-age students in the next decade. What was several years ago characterized as a continuing crisis in financing higher education will not slacken. Faculties are becoming increasingly tenure heavy because of legislation raising retirement ages and because there are fewer new jobs. There will be—most dangerous trend of all—less need for young faculty.

The mood, indeed all the imperatives, now point to contraction, self-sufficiency, a deepening of the pressure on faculty. Those pressures come and will continue to come most insistently from two quarters: from legislative or administrative cost-benefit analysis and productivity studies and from the increasing migration of students toward more immediately "practical" and vocationally oriented subjects. Thus the humanities feel and will continue to feel this double squeeze—to justify what they do and to give others skills they can "use"—more acutely than any other segment of the university world.

It will be a hard time. While it will be true, it will not be enough to advert to the dignity of man, the connectedness among things; the way the humanities prepare for life and sharpen critical judgment, and give a keener appreciation of experience; how they express, and teach us to express, the highest values we can live by; or the way they are valuable in and of themselves. The reason this will not do is that, under pressure, humanists, as well as others, did not really seem to believe it. Ten to twelve years ago, it was in many places the humanists, not the hard scientists or social scientists, but the humanists, or at least people who taught in humanities departments, who wrote the guidelines that displaced the requirements for a B.A., who eloquently undermined the writing and the foreign-language requirements, who instituted the grading reforms that, some would argue, did nothing to discourage other pressures that were inflating grades. You can call what happened then a new spirit of freedom; you can call it a vocational crisis; you can call it anything you wish. The fact remains that the humanists, self-proclaimed as central and vital links to all of experience, displaced themselves, said they were not necessary to an ordered existence, even when that existence was only undergraduate education, much less society's stream of life. And in seeming to will themselves to the periphery, humanists made themselves in subsequent hard financial times perilously vulnerable.

Early in May 1977, the faculty at a major state university in New England voted overwhelmingly for the removal of the President and the Provost, the cause for that series of votes being a plan presented by the Provost to cut a number of faculty positions and to excise two departments—Asian Studies and Slavic Languages. The language departments tend to be the first to go. The more remote, geographically, the sooner they feel the sword. When we come to European languages, it is always a nice question whether Portuguese or Italian will precede Classics when the cuts are imposed. It is an extraordinarily melancholy sight, the devastation of foreign languages in this country— the sliding enrollments and smaller and smaller numbers of faculty involuntarily justifying the analyses that proceed by the numbers. The demise of foreign languages is part of a larger assault on literacy, part of a larger decline in the capacity to handle any language at all. It is, I believe, a fact that in the last fifteen years, certainly the last ten, any American college student who knew anything about the dynamics of English—its struts and cables, its soaring spans, the way it holds together and works—knew it by analogy from the grammar of a foreign language. It is true, the old cliché that says a foreign language necessarily deepens one's grasp of one's native language. And what is true about language tends to be true of culture. All the general worry about students' capacity to structure and to express their thoughts in English must include the current sorry situation with foreign languages.

But what do we expect? When most college faculties in this country will not require either for admission or for graduation the knowledge of a foreign language, why should hard-pressed administrations think languages are crucial? If humanities faculties do not assert the mutual dependence and reliance of the various parts, then the parts, or some parts, will disappear. No one will articulate a coherent and useful view of the humanities if the humanists will not or cannot. And if the humanists do not, then what was threatened at that university I referred to, a situation where at the end of the twentieth century a student would not be able to study Russian or Chinese, or know people who were studying them, or be able to study them in translation from people who know the original, will be more and more the norm.

These remarks on foreign languages, whose plight is visible and whose position is central to the humanities, ought to be understood as including the arts, whose plight is not so visible but whose position within the humanities is no less central. These pursuits, music, theater, painting, sculpture, architecture, each with its own sign system or "language" and its own "texts," are very much a part of my view of the humanities. Here the values we think of as humanistic are given, by a private act of the imagination, public expression and exposure. The arts are particularly vulnerable, especially in institutions without professional schools of music or art or drama or architecture to act as buffers or lobbyists. These areas are vulnerable because their faculties, either performers or practitioners, often are not seen to have the clout they should have in "academic" circles; because while many students are drawn to the arts, many majors are not, and the numbers are low; and most fundamentally, because the arts are still viewed in many quarters, within the academy and without, as accidental, not essential, as ornamental, as something vaguely suspect, faintly interesting, and often useless, like exotic foreign languages. Again, unless humanities faculties and those sympathetic to them are willing and able to assert that the so-called creative or performing arts are as much a part of the way civilized life is ordered and given meaning as anything else is, then those pursuits may be hit and hit again. And so, eventually, will the allied faculties of musicology and the history of art, particularly at the graduate level, for the historical investigation of aesthetic objects is not especially valued where the aesthetic process has no real existence. We must not encourage such a view or appear to be unconcerned about its implications.

You may have noticed I refer in my remarks to humanities faculties, not humanities departments. Departments are often the bane as well as the prop of academic existence.

We complain about them, but we regard them as indispensable. You know we have been willing to vote to abolish grades, requirements, poverty, and war, but never departments. And yet I think that just as one cannot be captive, in order to survive, of attitudes of the recent past, so one cannot be captive of the administrative structures of the dimmer or dimmest past.

Departments were not brought down graven in stone. And no one wants, nor should one allow administrators, to define departments as if they were necessarily identical with areas of intellectual inquiry; or to regard areas of intellectual inquiry as if they were necessarily definable as departments. The ways people really think, teach, and especially do research are not defined solely by departments and never have been. Of course departments are necessary for bureaucratic and organizational purposes; of course they serve to indicate larger zones of concern and common interest, but they must be shaped and perhaps reconceived. Departments must be administered, but not as if they were sacraments.

Humanities departments must be thought of as forces in a field rather than feudal baronies. And the faculties that inhabit these departments must be willing to assert new administrative patterns, patterns that more nearly reflect the teaching and research interests of faculties, and the needs and desires of undergraduate and graduate students, than the present rigid, often arbitrary boundaries do. New administrative arrangements should not be allowed to grow like toadstools after summer rain—there has to be a vital, legitimate teaching interest to justify a new cluster or association of colleagues. But I am less worried about humanities departments undergoing rapid change than I am about seeing them atrophy and, because they cannot change in a time of vocational pressure, begin to wither away. My theme is simple: academic humanists must be flexible and choose to assert themselves, even if that means consolidation of resources, even if that means changing comfortable administrative structures, before choices are forced on them or, worse, before the power to choose is denied. If humanities faculties face their responsibilities and take the lead, they will be able to change and grapple with their futures. Otherwise, hard-pressed administrations may think they must lead by invoking some principal of pseudo-equity (Everything Is as Valuable as Everything Else) and slashing across the board.

What do I mean by new administrative patterns that better reflect how things are done? Simply, to revert to an earlier example, I mean larger language departments making common cause with smaller ones, instead of viewing everyone else as competition. To the extent it is feasible, language departments might begin to explore linguistics and its insights so that some levels and kinds of language teaching might be done in common through common techniques, rather than always by each department on its own. At the very least, some training in common procedures might be given to the graduate students who do the great bulk of undergraduate language instruction everywhere.

I am talking about literature departments pooling resources—which means teaching faculties and traditions—not to teach "comparative literature" but to teach "literature." I mean the organization of faculty members and courses by definable historical periods, rather than only by languages or thematic divisions; teaching in Classical Studies or Medieval Studies or Renaissance or Enlightenment or Modern Studies, or by cultural areas, like American or Afro-American Studies, and teaching and studying the art, history, literature, history of science, philosophy, religious thoughts of this grouping, rather than assuming that each discipline or subject is forever encased in the plastic bags of the departments. We must bring together the way faculties are organized and the way they teach and think.

Finally, I am thinking of humanities area programs— of placing, again, a language that has or will have a hard time by itself, alone, in the context of the philosophy and history and literature and art history of that language. Organize an area that way, and suddenly languages like the Slavic ones or German or Italian, or any number of others, look very different. Strong Classics departments that teach history, philosophy, archaeology, art, literature, numismatics, and papyrology, as well as the Greek and Latin languages, have always been area programs. Strong Classics departments have always been those fields of force that I would like to see us at least begin to explore as models. And these models might then be better able to explore those ways of affiliating with, and thus supporting and drawing support from, the social sciences. The insights of sociology and anthropology, of political and economic thought, of psychoanalysis are part of the way we think and teach and write. Let the curriculum follow the mind, not restrain it.

I think the humanities are definable by the kinds of materials they use; I think the humanists share common interpretive modes and angles of vision; I think connections, in innumerable ways, characterize our materials and our methods. I think common values, about humane order, a decent rationality, a spacious and civilizing flexibility, inform those materials and methods. I believe the humanities bear a tradition that is a spirit as well as a collection of texts and ways of seeing.

Humanities faculties must assert themselves. They must assert those affiliations, those common connections each to each, and assert them intellectually and administratively, in theory and in practice. If those who conceive of themselves as humanists—and they are not only academic people but all who believe in a shared core of values held by educated people through language—do not speak for themselves, no one else can or will.

⇜ *"Nature Justly Viewed"* ⇝

*T*ruly to be liberally educated, truly to be prepared to meet and shape the world of this century and the next, no man or woman can be without some grasp of the principles of scientific inquiry, the insights of scientific research, and the various languages that science speaks. There is a common fallacy of educational thinking that asserts that a liberal education is synonymous with the humanities. Nothing could be further from the truth. A liberally educated mind is precisely one that has composed itself sufficiently to experience the thrill, the deeply satisfying, rousing excitement, of seeing a mathematical solution move to the same kind of inevitable, economical fulfillment of itself as does a great sonnet; one that can derive the same pleasure from discerning and absorbing the nature of a pattern in matter as in a painting or in market behavior; that can find the same satisfaction in applying the results of technological experiments as in ap-

Freshman address, September 1979.

plying any other kind of knowledge, for the betterment of humankind. The imagination, the capacity to discover or impose a new shape with the mind, is the province of science as much as of any other form of human investigation. And the power of the imagination is finally the energy tapped and transformed by an education.

A college education can come in many settings, with many kinds of strengths. At Yale, it comes in the setting of a University College, which means that undergraduates are taught by those who also constantly and actively engage in graduate teaching and research. There is another common fallacy that asserts there is some inevitable and necessary conflict between teaching and research. Some would exalt teaching as if it could exist without research and would insist that the health of the College is separable from the University research pursuits of the faculty. I could not disagree more emphatically. Research, in whatever field, alone or in groups, done late at night or snatched at dawn, in laboratory, library, or at home, pursued for a few hours a day or throughout weekends, during vacations or on leave, is the essential source from which teaching is drawn. Indeed, the strength of Yale College derives in large part from the presence of the professional schools around it and from the fact the faculty of the College is also the faculty of the Graduate School. The needs of undergraduates are embraced by the same people who embrace their responsibilities to graduate students, to their professional disciplines, to themselves as scholars. The University is the universe in which the College exists, and the strength and coherence of the University College depend upon the collaboration of institutions and human efforts that make up the whole.

What, one might ask, does this *grand jeté* on the inseparability of teaching and research, undergraduate and graduate education, have to do with science, with what I said I was going to say? I think it has a good deal to do with it, in the following way. Science at Yale and the rise of research and graduate education at Yale followed nearly identical paths, the College giving rise to a graduate faculty that was essentially a science faculty, a science faculty that taught undergraduates and that included some of the most prominent figures American science has produced. Science at Yale came out of the heart of this place, the old brick row, just over a hundred years ago, and Yale science was at the heart of the development of professional education, and the advancement of knowledge, in America. It is a story that began in the middle of the last century and continues powerfully today.

In 1847 the Yale Corporation established the new Department of Philosophy and the Arts, independent of Yale College, meant to embrace science and the arts; that is, "philosophy, literature, history, the moral sciences, other than law or theology, the natural sciences excepting medicine and their application to the arts." The Department was created with two professorships, of agricultural and of practical chemistry, and began to offer courses in 1848. The most notable part of the Department was the Yale School of Applied Chemistry, described in the College Catalogue for 1847–48 as a "Laboratory on the College grounds to provide facilities for individual study and research by students other than undergraduates." Courses in the Department were offered in chemistry, metallurgy, agricultural science, and mathematics as well as in Greek, philology, Arabic, and Latin, but the great preponderance of students pursued science and engineering, the number of scientists, originally six in 1847, swelling to twenty-five by 1852.

In 1852 the Corporation approved a proposal to found a School of Engineering, and in the academic year 1854–55 the Trustees combined all theoretical and applied work into the Yale Scientific School. The School, the first of its kind, included the Department of Philosophy and the Arts, and, to the existing professorships in Chemistry, Natural History, Mathematics, and Physics were added new chairs in Civil Engineering, Metallurgy, and Analytical Chemistry. In the meantime, Mr. Joseph Sheffield was being urged by academics and townsmen alike to endow a scientific school; between 1858 and 1860 he gave handsomely of land, laboratory equipment, buildings, and endowment, and in 1861 the Sheffield Scientific School was established. In 1860, the University, as it by now had every right to be called, had decided to offer a Ph.D., and thus in 1861 occurred another notable event: the first Ph.D. degrees in America were awarded by Yale, one in classics, one in philosophy, one in astronomy. In 1862, another was given in classics; in 1863, two more in classics and one in engineering. These doctorates, particularly the first in science and engineering, grew out of the emphasis first put upon post-undergraduate research in the sciences.

Yale science continued to flourish, with another donor, George Peabody, giving "to promote the interests of Natural Science." The Peabody Museum was established in 1863, then as now one of the most distinguished centers of its kind in the country. The Peabody is one of Yale's glories and will, I trust, continue to develop in its critical role as a center for research and instruction and collegial stimulation in the physical, biological, and relevant social sciences as well as entertaining and instructing thousands of visitors annually. At the same time, from 1859 to 1871, Yale was adding chairs in Industrial Mechanics, Agriculture, Botany, Zoology, Mining, Palaeontology, Dynamical Engineering, and Mathematical Physics.

During these years, another strand of scientific research that would prove critical to the future of science and of science at Yale began to be woven into our fabric. In 1856, Samuel William Johnson was appointed Professor of Analytical Chemistry, and out of his teaching and work came the establishment of the Connecticut Agricultural Experiment Station on the Yale Campus in 1877; and from the research and teaching of his student Russell Chittenden came the leadership for a whole new field, known then as Physiological Chemistry, in which Chittenden took the first American Ph.D. from Yale, in 1880. Chittenden had begun teaching that subject in 1874, when he was an eighteen-year-old junior in the Sheffield Scientific School, and he held the first chair in Physiological Chemistry in America in 1882. He was joined twenty years later by his student Lafayette Mendel, and Mendel, with Thomas Burr Osborne of the Connecticut Agricultural Experiment Station, did pioneering work in protein chemistry, and on the dietary necessity of certain amino acids and of what became known as vitamins. Here is the field of biochemistry, in the words of Professor Joseph Fruton, to whom I am indebted for this account and much more, that "area of science in which there is a conscious interplay of chemistry—the study of the properties of molecules—and biology—the study of the properties of living things." The field has had various names—"Physiological Chemistry, Biological Chemistry, Chemical Biology, Cell Physiology, and, most recently, Molecular Biology"—and, as Professor Fruton reminds us, "began its existence as a university discipline in the United States just about 100 years ago, and Yale was its birthplace." As the present power and distinction of Yale's Department of Molecular Biophysics and Biochemistry and the allied research in the Department of Biology and the various departments of the Medical School all attest, this great tradition of leadership lives today.

The ancients believed places had geniuses who contained the spirit of a locale, and there were geniuses of the place in those days. I have alluded to some already, but two above all others deserve mention here for the science that they brought to Yale and that, through them, Yale took to America. The first is a towering figure, the two-hundredth anniversary of whose birth the University celebrates this year. He is Benjamin Silliman, the person most responsible for the establishment of science and graduate education in science at Yale and for bringing the Good News of science to early-nineteenth-century America. Born in Trumbull, Connecticut, in 1779, he entered Yale College at thirteen, graduated in 1796, and in 1802, at the age of twenty-three, was appointed Professor of Chemistry and Natural History. Silliman had intended to be a lawyer and had completed his legal apprenticeship, but his new position seized him, and, with characteristic vigor, he set about learning the subjects he would profess. He studied abroad in Philadelphia, London, and Edinburgh and in 1806 believed himself prepared to teach chemistry and metallurgy full-time.

Silliman served on the College faculty for fifty-one years, retiring at the age of seventy-four, in 1853. He remained a force, however, until his death at eighty-five, in 1864.

He oversaw the growth at Yale of chemistry, geology, metallurgy, natural history, mathematics, and engineering. He also nurtured the growth of science elsewhere, for beginning when he was fifty-five he lectured throughout the land for over twenty years on geology and chemistry. In Boston, fifteen hundred people twice a week came to hear him lecture in the Masonic Hall for up to two hours a session. Silliman annually lectured in New York and at the new Lowell Institute, near Boston, and in the next years went all over New England and the Western Reserve, to Pittsburgh, Baltimore, Charleston, Montgomery, Mobile, New Orleans, Natchez; when he was seventy-five, he lectured in St. Louis and, when he was seventy-seven, in Buffalo. He was a national figure, preaching for science in the service of God and man, an overwhelming presence, large, courtly, voluble, his lectures marked by spellbinding chemical experiments and by large drawings and specimens of rocks and fossils, his zest and oratory riveting, entertaining, and instructing thousands. Silliman himself recorded the best evaluation of this teaching when he notes that he heard one man say, "He's a smart old fellow," and his neighbor reply, "Yes, he is a real steamboat."

The human imagination, through science or anything else, can either discern a design or project a new principle. Silliman was a discerner. At Pittsburgh he said, "True science is fitted to teach us how the laws of nature are employed to produce the happy issue which everywhere present themselves to our admiring contemplation." His was not a speculative but an admiring genius, and he gloried in the Glory. When he was eighty-two, he wrote that in the study of science he had never forgotten to give honor to the Creator, "happy if I might be the honored interpreter of a portion of His works, and of the beautiful structure and beneficent laws discovered therein by the labors of many illustrious predecessors."

There is a moving generosity of spirit in these words as Silliman looked back at a lifetime of interpreting, through his textbooks, his lectures; through the *American Journal of Science and the Arts,* which he founded in 1818 and edited alone for twenty years; at the Department of Philosophy and the Arts, the School of Applied Chemistry, the Sheffield Scientific School; through the work of his pupils, and of his colleagues on the faculty including his son, Ben, and his son-in-law, the great naturalist, James Dwight Dana; at his work as a consulting chemist and geologist from Pennsylvania to Virginia; and at his role in organizing the American Geological Society and the American Association for the Advancement of Science. In Silliman's vision of the unity of knowledge—no separation between science and the arts; the mind of man an admiring model of the Creator's—in his reveling in the application of science to the cause and expansion of his beloved new country; as evangelist, entrepreneur, steamboat, and theologian of science, Silliman taught a nation to love the beauty and truth of what he called "nature justly viewed." And at the core of his love and belief was an educational vision that he first expressed just over one hundred and fifty years ago to the freshmen students in chemistry in Yale College, the vision of education as transcending simple utility and embracing knowledge for itself, a good from God. "It would now," he said in 1828, "be as disreputable for any person, claiming to have received a liberal education, or to possess liberal knowledge, to be ignorant of the great principles and of the leading facts of chemical as of mechanical philosophy." Courtly, shrewd, capacious Silliman—it would be hard to better that statement today and foolish to try.

And then there was another figure, who lived into our own century, also a graduate of and teacher at Yale, as different from Silliman as it was possible to be, not a discerner of design but a creator of principles, a deeply inward intellect whose clear and brooding reach, and capacity to imagine precisely and thorougly, makes him probably the greatest American scientist ever to live. I refer to Josiah Willard Gibbs. When President Day retired, in 1846, and his house became the School of Applied Chemistry, Day returned to his family residence on Crown Street; the family then occupying the Day House—Professor of Sacred Literature Josiah Gibbs and his wife, four daughters, and young son—built a home on High Street, where the younger Gibbs, save for three years of study in Paris, Berlin, and Heidelberg, would pass his whole life. At the age of ten, in 1849, Gibbs became a student at the Hopkins Grammar School, across the street from his home, where the Law School now stands, and at fifteen enrolled in Yale College, the College of the two Sillimans, Dana, and Gibbs's mentor, Hubert Anson Newton, Professor of Mathematics. In three of his four years at Yale, Gibbs took top prizes in Latin and mathematics. After graduating in 1858, he went on to obtain in 1863 the first American Ph.D. in engineering. He was a tutor in Latin and mathematics in the College for the next three years, and it is not completely fanciful, I think, to say that his gift for elegant composition in the ancient language fed his gift for compressed clarity—for elegance—in the language that is mathematics. Three years of European study in physics and mathematics built on his engineering and extended his theoretical grasp, and then Gibbs returned to Yale, to High Street, and spent his life as Professor of Mathematical Physics from 1871 until he died, in 1903. He went to his office in what became Farnam, he remained a bachelor, he rarely left New Haven again save for walking vacations in northern New England or New York, and he was buried in the Grove Street Cemetery, a block beyond the boyhood grammar school he served as trustee, two blocks from home.

What a modest, meticulous life, whose only outward pleasures were the picnics and suppers and outings of the Yale family, a lifelong gift for carpentry, and his science; what a contrast to Silliman, who wanted to scoop up the country in his hands and hold it up to the light. Silliman's opinions on religion, politics, science, the state of the Republic were nationally known; Gibbs's are, with the rarest exceptions, impossible to discover. Silliman was imperial, a portrait of him by Samuel F. B. Morse showing a figure that dominates the natural world he is demonstrating; Gibbs was reticent without shyness or hauteur, affable, deft, never absentminded or "otherworldly" but inward, concentrated. There are, however, virtues to such interiority. When Silliman hymned the great design, his utterances often passed rapidly from a solid to a gaseous state; Gibbs's always had a terrifying pellucid density, as he sought inexorably what he called several times the standpoint of greatest simplicity. Silliman was a geyser and a wonder to behold; Gibbs was a laser, who saw farther than anyone else of his time.

Martin J. Klein, Eugene Higgins Professor of the History of Physics and the country's leading historian of physics, has remarked that Gibbs's "laconic, mathematical" style made it difficult for all but the greatest of his contemporaries to understand what he was doing. But what Gibbs was doing, particularly in his three papers published in 1873 and 1878 in the *Transactions of the Connecticut Academy of Arts and Sciences,* was to extend and complete the field of classical thermodynamics and to give a foundation for the discipline of physical chemistry.

Gibbs's greatest work, done in his thirties, built on the theories concerning the transformation of energy into mechanical heat, developed by the German Rudolf Clausius and the Scotsman William Thomson, better known as Lord Kelvin. In 1873, Gibbs had seized on the concept of entropy, which determines the energy unavailable for work in a system. He had established that the fundamental thermodynamic equation for a system expressed its energy in terms of its entropy and volume, and from that essential insight flowed much of Gibbs's greatest work, in 1878, on the nature of equilibrium, work that, in the words of Professor Klein, "vastly extended the domain covered by thermodynamics, including chemical, elastic, surface, electromagnetic and electrochemical phenomena in a single system." His vision was boundless.

This massive and continuous act of the imagination, combining physics, mathematics, and chemistry, by a virtual unknown, in a small town in Connecticut, published in a journal of exceedingly limited circulation, came gradually to be recognized for the overwhelming achievement it was, and by the time its creator had published, at the end of his life, his great study of statistical mechanics, he was recognized for the genius that he was. Throughout it all, Gibbs had never wavered as a scientist or a man from the principle he expressed with characteristic conciseness in a letter to the American Academy of Arts and Sciences in 1881 accepting its prestigious Rumford Medal: "One of the principal objects of theoretical research in any department of knowledge is to find the point of view from which the subject appears in its greatest simplicity."

How great a scientist was Gibbs? My capacities are exhausted by asking the question. But I can report the answer implicit in the comment of one supremely qualified to judge. At the end of his life, Albert Einstein was interviewed by the Canadian scientist A. V. Douglas. "There remained," writes Douglas, "one special thing I wanted to ask him. Who were the greatest men, the most powerful thinkers whom he had known? The answer came back without hesitation, 'Lorentz.' . . . 'But,' he added. 'I never met Willard Gibbs; perhaps had I done so, I might have placed him beside Lorentz.' "

Gibbs, Silliman, and the others belong to all of science, theoretical and applied, and to its ongoing life, and I hope that my amateur's account does not carry a tone excessively parochial, for parochialism would more than anything contravene the spirit and substance of their achievements as scientists. And yet we at Yale should take a justifiable pride in the contributions these scientists have made, and their successors continue to make, to this place and to the country; we should not be cautious about celebrating them and what they stood for, or in finding satisfaction that they and their latter-day colleagues nourish, with so many others, the educational aspirations of our University.

And let us remember that those scholars who worked so hard to found the scientific school and the Ph.D., who established Yale, through science and other subjects, as a

University, also taught in a College, many remaining on its faculty, all encouraging the younger students. That fluidity of passage by members of the faculty between undergraduate and graduate teaching, between research and formal instruction; that accessibility, that concern for the community of ideas and healthy disregard of boundaries—where they only impede the pursuit of learning—is what comes through most clearly in the rise of science and graduate research at Yale. And that spirit, which turned a College into a University and forged the University College of a particular kind, that spirit of collaboration among people and ideas, continues to be the hallmark of this place and is one of the many gifts the science faculties of Yale bring to the institution. For this historical outline is really the outline of a continuing tradition here; you will find some of the most innovative teaching at Yale among the scientists, and among those most distinguished nationally for research in science there is often the clearest sense of the educational needs of the young student. This spirit shaped by scientists over a century ago retains its force today.

From the scientists, social and natural, we derive our belief in the unifying force of the search for knowledge, and in the harmonies among forms of knowledge, even as knowledge, increasing, tends to fragment itself and us with it. From them we learn what we should never forget, that to view nature justly, nature human and material, we must eschew parochialism and casual labels and bureaucratic boundaries and seek to see the truth from as many vantage points as humankind can summon. That search for ways of seeing the truth humanely and wholly is the role of a great university.

NOTE: I have drawn heavily on various sources in this essay, and none must be blamed for whatever vagaries of interpretation or errors are contained herein. For the rise of science in graduate education, I have relied on Edgar S. Furniss, *The Graduate School at Yale: A Brief History* (New Haven: 1965), and for these matters and Silliman on *Benjamin Silliman and His Circle: Studies on the Influence of Benjamin Silliman on Science in America,* ed. Leonard G. Wilson (New York: Science History Publications, 1979), particularly the essays of Wilson, John C. Greene, and Louis I. Kuslan. The citations from Silliman, Sr., are drawn from Greene's essay. For Gibbs, I have used the basic biography by Lynde Phelps Wheeler, *Josiah Willard Gibbs: The History of a Great Mind* (New Haven and London: Yale University Press, 1952), and, most of all, have drawn heavily on the goodwill and scholarship of Professor Martin J. Klein, particularly his essay "Gibbs on Clausius," in Russell McCormmach, ed., *Historical Studies in the Physical Sciences,* vol. 1 (Philadelphia: University of Pennsylvania Press, 1969), pp. 127–49; his contribution on Gibbs to the *Dictionary of Scientific Biography* (New York: Scribner, 1972), 5:386–93; and his "The Early Papers of J. Willard Gibbs: A Transformatin of Thermodynamics" (paper presented at the Fifteenth International Congress of the History of Science, 1977), now published in revised form in *Human Implications of Scientific Advance,* ed. E. G. Forbes (Edinburgh: Edinburgh University Press, 1978). Professor Klein also kindly provided me with the passage from the Douglas interview with Einstein, "Forty Minutes with Einstein," *Journal of the Royal Astronomical Society of Canada* 50 (1956): 99. I am also indebted to Joseph S. Fruton, Eugene Higgins Professor of Biochemistry, for allowing me to use material from his unpublished paper on the history of biochemistry at Yale, presented to the Department of Molecular Biophysics and Biochemistry, April 9, 1979.

»» *Yale and Athletics* ««

As is customary, we can discover how we think about ourselves by looking at how we speak about ourselves. Two words of ancient Greek, *athlōn* and *athlōs*, shape a third, *athletēs*. *Athlōs* meant a contest; *athlōn*, a prize won in a contest; and they provide us with *athletēs*, an individual competing for a prize in the public games. Here in small compass is much of the ancient Greek world. Life and all that is valuable is seen as a contest. Struggle and contention lie at the core of everything, and one must devote all one's being to winning. If one wins, there is a prize, a tangible mark of triumph in the endless competition. Merit, skill, capacity—call it what you will— must be tested and, if victorious, rewarded.

No part of Greek life was immune to this view of competition or to the possibility of triumph. If you won a footrace or a chariot race, you could ask Pindar to immortalize

Delivered in a longer version to the Association of Yale Alumni, April 1980.

your achievement in an ode; if you were Aeschylus or Sophocles or Euripides, and you won the annual three-day contest for dramatists in Athens, you gained a prize. By the fifth century B.C., what we would call the realms of the athletic and the artistic were not separate in the intensity of competition or in the assumption that reward would follow victory or in the importance placed on the activities by the culture. The athlete and the artist lived in the same world and did the same thing: they both asserted the spirit in order to thrust the individual beyond time and achieve something permanent.

A sense of proportion between the exertions of body and mind was essential to the shaping of a triumph or a life, and this perspective is concisely expressed in the dialogue between Socrates and Glaucon in the third book of Plato's *Republic*. Socrates sums it up:

> . . . it seems there are two arts which I would say some god gave to mankind, music and gymnastics, for the service of the high-spirited and the love of knowledge in them— not for the soul and body incidentally, but for the harmonious adjustment of these two principles by the proper degree of tension and relaxation of each. (412)

An earlier, Homeric ethos of winning at any cost was transmuted by Plato's time into a strict observance of the rules and a deep sense that the law was essential to survival. The toughness, however, of their ancestors remained part of the Greek soul that Plato was so concerned to reform; for while Plato asserted physical training and games as explorations of knowledge of the spirit on behalf of a healthy citizen and healthy state, he never considered athletics as pleasurable in itself. Nor did he have any idea of sportsmanship, or of what we call character building. In Plato, physical training and games are part of the necessary regimen that will make a soul shapely and balanced and thus defend it against impurities, and defend a city against its enemies. The concept of athletics as important for creating other values, of teamwork, moral character, social equity, comes as a legacy from nineteenth-century England.

The English before the nineteenth century enjoyed sport—some bloody, some not, but in most cases unorganized. Only somewhat over a century ago, in the 1850s and 1860s, were the rules of many games codified, with the rules of Rugby football having been set in 1846. That game carries the name of a great English public school, and in 1858 Thomas Hughes wrote an immensely successful and influential novel about a boy at Rugby. Called *Tom Brown's School Days,* the novel presented a Rugby where games were the heart of school life and of the making of a brother in what came to be called the fellowship of muscular Christians.

A Master in *Tom Brown's School Days* says of cricket that the "discipline and reliance on one another, which it teaches, are so valuable." In an educational philosophy where character is more important than intellect and teamwork more valued than individuality, games are the teachers; the school is simply the place where the games happen. By midcentury, as Asa Briggs has said, games are "institutions," and on the fields of those institutions develop ideals of sportsmanship, and fair play, and team spirit, and the development of character for later life, which are still with us. How different are those from the Greek ideals. The Greeks saw physical training and games as a form of knowledge, meant to toughen the body in order to temper the soul; activities pure in themselves, immediate, obedient to the rules so that winning would be sweeter still. The English ideals, on the other hand, aim beyond the field to the battleground of life, and they emphasize fellowship, sacrifice, a sense that how one plays is an emblem of how one will later behave; they teach that victory is ultimately less important than the common experience of struggling in common. Discipline and a view of life as a contest are part of both attitudes, but the two concepts of the value and purpose of athletics are as different as they can be, as different as exalting a shining, individual winner, and cherishing a character that effaces itself in the team.

We inherit these distinct views of athletics, each with its own aspects of cult, each placing athletics within an educational framework, each devoted to an amateur ideal. The two views are held in common by individuals and by institutions to this day, but they coexist uneasily. That ambivalence exists within our own Ivy Group—those institutions most closely modeled on the English public schools and universities, where organized collegiate competition grew up in America in the nineteenth century—and that ambivalence is easily stated: does one place the highest value on winning, or does one subordinate victory to the larger values of an educational institution? We think we have chosen the latter idea, but we are nervous, nervous because we do not want to lose at anything, any more than Tom Brown, or Frank Merriwell, did. The ambivalence about how to merge winning and education is writ large in the country's ambivalence about big-time collegiate athletics. It was obvious in the national debate about the 1980 Summer Olympics—the Greeks among us, believing in their individual destinies, wanted to go to Moscow and win; the Anglo-Saxons among us, team members all, played along with President Carter.

Where does Yale stand in 1980? Do organized games and physical training have any role in our modern University, and if they do, what are their purposes? If my sketch of how athletics has come to us is valid, it is clear that we behave like the English and think like the Greeks. But to create a contest between the ancients and the moderns and then to stand as spectators at the match trying to decide which side to root for is not enough. We must know if athletics figures in our educational scheme and, if so, how. I believe that athletics is part of an education of a young person, as the Greeks and the English schoolmasters believed: and I believe athletics is part of an education because athletics teaches lessons valuable to the individual by stretching the human spirit in ways that nothing else can. Is there a view of education that will contain this conviction concerning athletics?

There is, and I can offer it in no better way than by citing one of the subtlest and most powerful minds of the nineteenth century, another Englishman who thought profoundly about the nature of education. I refer to John Henry Cardinal Newman and *The Idea of a University*. In the fifth discourse of that work, Cardinal Newman distinguishes "liberal" education from "servile" or useful education. "[T]here are bodily exercises," he says, "which are liberal, and mental exercises which are not so."[*] Those

---

[*] Citations throughout are from the 1968 edition of Holt, Rinehart and Winston, New York.

pursuits that are intellectual and not liberal are those of a professional or commercial education. He then turns to exercises of the body that are, in his sense, liberal.

> Such, for instance, was the palaestra, in ancient times; such the Olympic games, in which strength and dexterity of body as well as of mind gained the prize. In Xenophon we read of the young Persian nobility being taught to ride on horseback and to speak the truth; both being among the accomplishments of a gentleman.

And what is the conceptual grounding that allows for this view of physical training as "liberal"? "[T]hat alone is liberal knowledge," says Newman,

> which stands on its own pretensions, which is independent of sequel, expects no complement, refuses to be *informed* (as it is called) by any end, or absorbed into any art, in order duly to present itself to our contemplation. The most ordinary pursuits have this specific character, if they are self-sufficient and complete; the highest lose it, when they minister to something beyond them.

Newman drew upon Aristotle and other Greek thinkers to go beyond them, and to develop a view of a liberal education that also had his own culture's stamp upon it. We recognize that stamp when he says that education is higher than instruction because education "implies an action upon our mental nature, and the formation of a character." Various philosophies of education, therefore, come together in Newman's idea of a liberal education, and various notions of athletics cluster, too, in the larger vision here projected so powerfully.

Such an ideal of education, and of the proper place of athletics within it, should be with us to this day, in this place, and must shape our thinking. Such a liberal education, properly understood, supports athletics as an essential part of the educational process. It is equally consistent with this view, however, that athletics not outstrip that larger process, or deviate from it. Such an ideal means that we no more encourage a professionalism of spirit in athletics in our undergraduates than we encourage a professional view of the purpose of an undergraduate education. It means we believe in an education that is a process of exploration and fulfillment, not a process of pursuing a career.

Consistent with this perspective is Plato's idea of the necessity for proportion in things of the spirit. And thus we must remember that it is our obligation to consider our students as students above all else, and to treat them in an evenhanded fashion, and to construct their athletic programs so that their time to develop as thinking and feeling human beings is not deformed by the demands of athletic pursuits. The time and effort given to athletics by a student must be proportioned in such a way that the student has more time and energy for studies than for sports. Yale is not the place for Tom Brown; his Rugby and Oxford had their still air broken often by the cries of players but never by the rustling of a page. There must be at Yale, in philosophy and in actuality, proportion in how the institution shapes itself and in how it encourages and sanctions a student's behavior. Athletics is essential but not primary. It contributes to the point, but it is not the point itself.

By *athletics* in what follows, I mean formal sports systematically pursued, physical training and physical recreation. In thinking about athletics this way, one realizes immediately that many more people than students are involved. And therefore while it is appropriate to have a view of athletics within education for undergraduates, and we do, we must also remember that there are an equal number of graduate and professional students at Yale. For many of them, various forms of athletics are important. Within the University community, there are also postdoctoral students, staff, faculty, alumni, and the spouses of all these people, for whom access to and use of activities and facilities are important. Athletics generously conceived, therefore, touches thousands throughout the Yale community. When we construct principles according to which the University will allocate its resources for athletics, we must place an educational vision at the core, but we must also remember that it is a community of people larger than any student body. In constructing principles, we must remember also that Yale's physical facilities for athletics need their share of resources, else a distinguished physical asset will continue to deteriorate and a whole community will be impoverished. Finally, we need always to recall that the production of revenue is as much a part of the picture of Yale athletics as the provision of services and opportunities. Yet, as we seek actively to increase revenue so that growing expenses can be borne, we must be extraordinarily careful. We cannot increase revenues by exploiting students simply as athletes, or by allowing others to displace members of the Yale community for whom the physical resources are first intended. Most important, we cannot do anything to increase revenue that would in any way impair the educational mission of the University.

The University's commitment to athletics as part of the larger nature and purpose of the University informs the following principles that guide and will guide the University as it thinks of athletics and as it allocates scarce resources to athletics.

The first principle, already implicitly set forth, is that there must be a broadly based program of athletic opportunities, of a competitive and noncompetitive sort, on a variety of levels. We must sustain a broad program that allows for formal and informal physical activity, by individuals and by groups, at all seasons, for all purposes. America needs citizens who know how to cherish fitness of the body along with fitness of the mind.

The second principle, focused on Yale College, follows from the first, and it is that the intramural program for athletics within the residential-college system must be nourished and sustained. The residential colleges are essential to an education in Yale College. They are far more than simply residences because of the energy of the academic, literary, musical, theatrical, social, and athletic life contained within them, and they provide intelligible, manageable communities for advising, teaching, learning, and life. The intramural competition among the colleges is a critical element in the system's success.

My third principle speaks to a specific type of athletic activity: we must encourage a group of varsity sports that aspire to high intercollegiate achievement within the context of the Ivy Group. Yale currently [1980] has thirty-seven varsity sports squads, the largest number offered by an institution in the Ivy Group. In this area, we must strive to do what we do well, by providing coaching, which is to say, teaching, of the highest quality, facilities and equipment adequate to the needs and talents of the students involved, and an atmosphere of aspiration to excellence within the spirit of a liberal education and the context of the Ivy Agreement of 1954.

Varsity sports are important, though not more important than intramural athletics or the broad program of opportunities offered the whole community. We must recognize that varsity athletics is the most expensive part of the total athletic program, and we must find appropriate ways to increase the revenue flowing from varsity sports. We must also recognize that it will doubtless be necessary to do fewer things, in this area of Yale as in others, in order to do what we do as well as possible.

In thinking about varsity athletics, we must understand that coaching is crucial and that the highest standard of coaching must be sought here as it must be sought in all other programs of a teaching nature in the university. I believe it must be widely acknowledged as well that recruiting is not coaching, and that the present practice of the recruitment of students who are athletes cannot encroach upon the time and effort that must be devoted to working with the students who are here, working with them and teaching them in one form or the other. I will return to this point later.

We all know that varsity athletics is the most visible part of the athletics program. It is the one some alumni, and others, find most immediately available as a form of connection with Yale. When a program in History of Physics or Divinity or Nursing is lessened or dropped, the people who think most fondly of Yale in terms of the Departments of History or Physics, or the Schools of Divinity or Nursing, do not feel as immediately betrayed as alumni and others seem to when the same process of necessary, and carefully considered, reduction goes on among varsity sports. In short, pressure groups flare up quickest in this area. And yet, if we insist, as I do, that athletics is essential to the larger educational program and purposes of Yale, then athletics at all levels cannot expect to be immune to the pressures afflicting all the other parts of the University. With regard to varsity athletics, some changes will continue to be made so that we can afford to do what we will do at the level of excellence Yale must expect.

I often bring up won-lost records in assessing the health of varsity athletics because I want there to be no doubt about what I believe. I think winning is important. Winning has a joy and discrete purity to it that cannot be replaced by anything else. Winning is important to any man's or woman's sense of satisfaction and well-being. Winning is not everything, but it is something powerful, indeed beautiful, in itself, something as necessary to the strong spirit as striving is necessary to the healthy character. Let all of us without bashfulness assert what the Greeks would find it absurd to suppress. Having said that, and meaning it, I repeat what I said above: our commitment to excellence, of aspiration and achievement, is based on the basic presupposition that athletics plays a properly proportioned role within our educational philosophy and program.

Our fourth principle in making athletic decisions is that there must be opportunities for instruction and competition in a wide variety of physical skills. I have referred already to our programs and resources in physical education and to our commitment to individual recreation. There are others. We may well find that some varsity sports can be sustained only at a sub-Ivy level of competition, with part-time coaching or schedules that do not involve great amounts of travel. We ought also to remember that Yale fields eighteen club sports, ranging from badminton through Frisbee to women's rugby. Club sports are the result of student initiative; the Department of Athletics, Physical Education, and Recreation provides no administrative or technical support—that is, it does not schedule contests or provide coaches—but it does offer modest funding for equipment and travel. The club program is inexpensive; it is important as a way of providing an outlet for genuine interest without an elaborate administrative superstructure. Newman's ideal of the self-contained liberal pursuit fits the club activities elegantly.

Does Yale really care about athletics? The answer is unequivocally yes, Yale does care and will care; Yale cares enough to assert that athletics plays a vital part in the education of its young people and in the ongoing life of everyone else. As a sign of its commitment to athletics, Yale will treat athletics according to the same central educational values and with the same desire for excellence that it brings to its other essential parts.

After this look at our educational philosophy, at the principles and priorities established for athletics, where are we? We are ready for the future. And the future, while it will build on our strengths, also presents us with problems.

I believe that we have problems with regard to the Ivy

Agreement of 1954. While every Ivy institution observes the financial aid policies set forth in that agreement, there are other areas where we have drifted away from the original statement. Because I believe this to be so, and because I believe Yale should be in the lead in reaffirming the spirit and intent of the basic Ivy Agreement, I took to my fellow presidents in the Ivy Group in December 1979 a set of proposals and positions designed to bring us back to the basic principles. These proposals, now being studied by the Policy Committee of the Ivy Group, represent four areas where I intend to press as hard as I can for revision and reform. In these areas, I believe there is a lack of proportion, an imbalance, in the way the programs in athletics in the Ivy Group have been allowed to grow. The result of this disproportion is, in my opinion, that some students, and not a trivial number, spend far, far too much time, with the encouragement of the institutions, on athletic pursuits; the result is that coaching has gone a long, long way, particularly in some sports, to being a matter of recruiting and not of teaching; the result is that athletics in the Ivy Group now hungers for that next event, that sequel, that bigger-league look and feel, that I think violates the essence of what we believe the role of organized athletics in our institutions ought to be. If the Ivy Group wants to be more than a set of financial aid policies and a concatenation of schedules, then I think it must return to its first principles. Else, as a group and as individual institutions, we will lose precisely what is liberating and fulfilling in our kind of college athletics, and we will gain nothing save the scorn of those who wonder why we act in a fashion so inconsistent with our ideals and principles.

The proposals I made to my colleagues are the following:

We must, as a Group, discuss the restricting of recruiting by coaches to on-campus conversations and visits. It is, in my judgment, wrong to spend more for off-campus recruiting of students who are also athletes than is spent on the recruitment of students in general. Nor is it acceptable to the spirit of my proposal to designate an officer in the central admissions office as having a special, full-time responsibility for the recruitment of athletes. We all must recruit students for our institutions nationally, but I do not believe we should send our coaches to recruit students who are athletes as a special group. The present practices now pursued in varying ways everywhere only tend to create separate groups of students; these practices only escalate the competition for stars; they only force more and more of coaching to become hustling in the hustings. As I have said, coaching is teaching—valuable, honorable, and difficult. I believe it is demeaning to the profession of coaching when one has to spend so much time traveling and wooing off-campus.

We must, as a Group, cease to think of postseason competition in any varsity sport as the natural or even necessary consequence of victory. The Ivy Group championship must be the goal of our students, and where the Ivy championship is not the major goal, or is a figment only of the daily press's imagination, the status of Ivy championships must be elevated and affirmed. What I find so injurious to our principles and to the education of our students is the pressure to prepare for the next step, the amount of time and effort expended to get ready for what follows the regular season, the insidious sense that there is nothing valuable in the experience of being first-rate within your own league and that one has to complete some sequence to the national level. I am frankly not impressed with the argument that says, Why can't we be excellent (or, you say we should be excellent), and therefore why can't we test ourselves against the best? Yale students are among the best; they are tested, and will be tested, with the best all their lives. It is to misconceive a Yale education, however, to think that education is intended simply to be the setting for a national-level athletic career in anything. If athletic gifts are there, and they blossom after graduation, fine. But Yale is not the place to come if the purpose of coming is to spend disproportionate amounts of time on athletics in order to compete beyond the Ivy Group while in college.

• I genuinely believe in Newman's ideal of a liberal education, an education designed at its heart not for what comes next but for the fulfillment of the pursuit, and the person, in and of itself. The spirit of postseason competition, in my view, violates that principle, whether that principle is construed as general to education or as specific to athletics.

We must, as a Group, reexamine our schedules of practice and of play in athletics, in terms of both their length and their scope. In the Ivy Group, I think we have in general regulated football well, and I say that knowing that I think ten games to a season is one too many and that a preseason scrimmage, adding in effect one more game, should not be allowed. I cannot, however, express the same confidence at all with regard to other sports, like hockey and basketball. In those, and others, we play at the varsity level seasons that I think are too long and schedules that move way beyond the Ivy Group into a staging area for national competition. Needless to say, I find such situations consistent with neither our educational principles nor our students' educational needs. I believe a number of sports need examination in terms of their schedules of practice and play at the highest level of the Ivy Group.

We must, as individual institutions, if not as a Group, explore seriously the practice of multiseasonal coaching assignments, that is, of requiring coaches to span more than one athletic season. If I am told that a given season begins too early or ends too late to allow such an arrangement, then my reply is that the season is probably too long; if I am told that a coach may have obligations with his players after the normal end of a season, then my reply is that we should not allow postseason competition; and if I am told that travel occupies, necessarily, a great deal of a coach's time after the season, then my reply is that we should not require, or allow, off-campus recruiting by coaches. My point is that coaches *are* teachers and that they must not be made into something else by the multiple pressures brought about by present recruitment practices, postseason opportunities, and swollen schedules. Gifted coaches, and there are many, can and ought to work with students in various contexts. Members of the faculty do; it is part of the pleasure, part of the job, part of the profession.

My first three proposals, in particular, are in areas where I believe the Ivy institutions must act in concert. They need to act together for two reasons: it is impossible for one institution to act unilaterally and still remain in the Group in any realistic or practical sense; and these institutions, having agreed to place athletics within similar educational programs, governed by a similar philosophy, must act in concert if they wish to affirm the integrity not only of their athletic activities but also of their larger programs and of that liberal philosophy.

Within an overall philosophy of education, the Ivy Group wants to combine, in athletics, training of skills and character with a joy in winning. I believe all the Ivy institutions want this, and I believe it is a right and proper thing to want. I am convinced that if we go back to the first principles and to the spirit of our Agreement, we will find again, through common effort, a structure for the educational values, the sense of proportion in athletics, and the sheer pleasure in hard competition among ourselves that we all want, and none of us wants to lose.

For my part, I commit Yale toward that end. It is a goal consistent with our belief in athletics as important to the educational program of our students and to the healthy life of our whole community. It is a goal consistent with our deepest conviction concerning a liberal education and a necessary proportion in a civilized, fruitful life. There is a strong spirit at Yale, a strong spirit compounded of respect for the glories of mind and body striving in harmony; and let there be no doubt about what we have affirmed or any doubt about what we have projected. The educational ideals and principles that I have asserted must *be* Yale's athletic policy; they must be like a seamless garment, for it is our students and their education that are finally at issue. It is our students for whom our principles and beliefs are intended; it is our students who deserve a place with purpose and proportion. It is our students in whom the spirit that is Yale will live, and it is they who most deserve to know upon what ground of belief we stand, and why we have chosen to stand there.

⇶ *The State of the College Game* ⇷

John Henry Newman's vision[*] is one to ⸱
inspire us still, where the discrete, self-contained character
of the pursuit, physical or mental, is the essence; where
the lack of expectation of sequel, the absence of a goal
except the enactment of the pursuit itself, makes the pursuit
a liberal one. Thus, an athletic contest construed as enjoy-
able in itself, with no expectation of a consequence beyond
the playing of it, as hard and as fully as possible, is a
natural and inevitable part of a program of education
called, in Cardinal Newman's (and my) terms, "liberal."

Such an ideal of education, and of the proper place of
athletics within it, should be with us to this day. Such a
liberal education, properly understood, supports athletics
as an essential part of the educational process. It is equally
consistent with this view, however, that athletics not out-

Delivered at Williams College, September 1987.

[*] See "The Earthly Use of a Liberal Education" and "Yale and Athletics."

strip that larger process, or deviate from it. Such an ideal means that we no more encourage a professionalism of spirit in athletics in our undergraduates than we encourage a professional view of the purpose of an undergraduate education. It means we believe in an education that is a process of exploration and fulfillment, a love of learning for its own sake, not a process of technical training for pursuing a career.

This is the basic assumption with which I begin. In what follows, I make other assumptions: for instance, by *athletics* I mean organized sports for students as fostered and sanctioned by the institution—not physical education or recreation.

Because I assume athletics is an important part of a collegiate education, I believe athletics ought to be subject to the same scrutiny as other parts of the educational institution are. The tragedy of much of today's intercollegiate athletic scene is that a significant number of institutions believe that athletics means only certain revenue-producing sports, and only at the varsity level. I believe as well in junior varsity and club and intramural athletics, in a wide variety of sports, available to all interested and able students.

An institution that truly believes that athletics is important to overall education strives, within its limits, to provide a broadly based, broadly participatory program for students. I assume it is at least open to debate whether an institution that supports only six or seven revenue-producing varsity teams truly believes athletics is important. One of my assumptions is that such "big-time" institutions are interested in something else—marketing the institutions to regents, legislators, alumni; producing revenue to support the athletic program or, perhaps, academic programs;[*] leaving unchallenged the idea, so dear to the media, particularly television, that athletic excellence and academic excellence are a function of each other.

Of course, there is no necessary correlation—one way or the other—between "big-time" athletic excellence and "big-time" academic excellence. Excellence in one area indicates neither excellence in the other nor necessary weakness. We should purge ourselves of the sentimental notions on both sides, either that Old Siwash is a great university because it is great at sport X; or that Old Siwash must be a weak academic institution because it has a strong athletic program. Two of the greatest—most excellent, deepest, strongest, most innovative—universities in America, and the world, are Stanford University and the University of Chicago. Their very different athletic programs tell us a great many admirable things about each place but cannot be taken as simple indices to the world-class stature of those two places as academic institutions.

There are several overlapping contexts in which my assumptions operate. Let me begin by describing a composite meeting of a group of academic administrators. A great pharmaceuticals company has proposed to the university a two-million-dollar grant to support basic research in neurology. Present are six or seven people—the Provost or Vice-Chancellor, the Dean of the Graduate School, the Dean of the Medical School, a high-level administrator concerned with grants and contracts, perhaps the University

[*] Despite the oft-made claim that big-time sports revenue is essential to the academic mission, is there a library or laboratory or classroom anywhere that was built from the revenue derived from selling undergraduate athletes to television?

General Counsel, perhaps some very senior faculty from the Sciences with administrative responsibility. Often the President of the university is in the meeting. The meeting has occurred often in the past dozen years in this country in many universities. The subject is private-sector sponsorship of research. The afternoon lengthens as the issues are discussed. They include the following:

- How to manage the company's need to treat knowledge as property and the university's need to provide free access to, and open discussion of, the results of research. Knowledge as property versus knowledge as a free good.

- How to define a senior faculty researcher's relationship to the company as a consultant while maintaining the principle of the university's overriding claim on its faculty for teaching, research, and citizenship. How to manage, in short, potential conflicts of time and of commitment.

- And finally, and most vexing because it is least susceptible to principled guidelines, how to ensure that graduate students and postdoctoral students will be protected so that they may continue to be trained to seek out results wherever their scientific gifts will take them, and not be subtly drawn to projects, or be assigned projects, that are designed to benefit only the eventual commercial needs of the sponsoring company. How, in short, to fulfill the research arrangement without commercializing the training of students. How to satisfy the differing but equally legitimate corporate imperatives of the company and the university.*

---

* See "Free Market and Free Inquiry."

Such conversations go on all the time; genuine issues are engaged, and mutually principled and agreeable arrangements are often arrived at. The reason for the care with which an institution should examine, in an open and sensitive fashion, the issues sketched here, and the many issues each of these points entails, is that any college or university has multiple responsibilities—to cooperate appropriately with various sectors of society; to safeguard the values and the rights of faculty, students, and staff; to do what it can uniquely to further knowledge for the betterment of human life; to define its responsibilities and prerogatives as an institution, and to maintain its own environment. The environment of a college or university marked by competition—competition within itself and between and among people, among ideas, for resources, with other institutions. But this is a competitive world that, in the interests of maintaining cohesion and civility, cherishes noncompetitive values. It cherishes the noncompetitive values of freedom from the need to achieve short-term results or immediate utility and of freedom from proprietary claims or the contention over property rights. A college or university is a paradox in many ways; perhaps the deepest paradox, and the most delicate balance to be struck, is the need to foster the competition of ideas, so that the best may emerge, while not allowing individuals to be crushed or corroded, so that humanity and decency prevail.

It is in the service of that total environment—to foster debate, disagreement, dissent, and the open exchange of ideas while requiring decent and civil relations, free of manipulation or coercion or secrecy—that the long meeting is held. This account is not intended to convince you that colleges and universities *alone* go through such considerations, for many kinds of corporate entities undergo such examinations internally, in ways appropriate to their ethical standards and responsibilities. Nor is it intended to convince you of the efficiency of colleges and universities, for they sacrifice efficiency for consensus all the time. It is, rather, a scene described to show that where large amounts of money or financial incentives are involved, educational institutions should and must take every care to meet their multiple responsibilities to all the people they serve—students, faculty, staff, sponsors, society.

Why, then, do so many universities—so scrupulous at the level of research, so concerned for policy and procedure when dealing with sponsorship for research teams of senior faculty and of postdoctoral and graduate students—assert and maintain *no* comparable standards for undergraduates? Why no protections against commercializing nineteen-year-olds?

Why no such care for people and principle when making a television deal for football? That, too, is a form of corporate sponsorship, involving millions of dollars. It is bizarre behavior.

Before two universities sued in federal court and won the right for each institution to make its own deal, with cable or network, institutions made their arrangements with television through the NCAA, the same body, set up by colleges in 1906, to regulate intercollegiate athletics, to monitor abuses, to oversee the college athletic landscape. The NCAA was in an impossible bind—meant to regulate the behavior of institutions it negotiated for; meant to set the number of athletic scholarships and to get the best television deal. The NCAA is not entirely to blame for the sorry state of much of big-time athletics, although its mechanisms for monitoring are weak. Nor is television entirely to blame. Television is in the entertainment business and is in search of product.*

I blame those responsible for running the offending colleges or universities that a number of institutions are the minor-league clubs for the NFL and the NBA; that there is a scandalous set of arrangements everyone knows about whereby young people are given money—regardless of whether they need it—to attend some school for the sole purpose of playing a sport for the commercial gain of the institution. The blame lies with the academic leadership, not with evil external forces.

It is *their* students who are often segregated in separate but equal or better housing; who have often special academic tutors and program of study; who may lose their scholarship or grant-in-aid if they are injured and therefore unable to play; who are expected to fulfill four years of eligibility (often taking five years in the practice called red-shirting) but not four years of course work; who are recruited specially; who are often admitted outside the normal admissions process. These students are not subjected to the same norms, expectations, and academic requirements as other students. They have perpetrated upon

---

* I find the smarmy pieties of certain television sportscasters who do college football games repulsive, as they alternately decry the state of big-time sports in their client universities and then run as much college football as late into the year, in as many contrived bowls, as possible. It is of a piece with television's habit, when televising professional football, of flashing on the screen the college or university a player attended, thus perpetuating the illusion that this is just a game for big boys; perpetuating the illusion that there is some connection between education and professional expertise at football; perpetuating the illusion that the majority of the pro athletes shown have graduated from college, when they have not. But television is in the business of illusions, and *caveat receptor*.

them—by the very educational institution that makes money off them, increases its fame because of them, and does not educate them or give them the space and time to educate themselves—a cruel hoax: they are called students, meant to receive an education, when they are in reality mercenaries. Extraordinary, and extraordinarily intense, schedules of weight-training, practice, and play, including travel and public appearances, make a mockery of the claim that an education is even at issue or that, without the athletic scholarship, so-and-so would not obtain a college education. Has so-and-so obtained a college education? Has he or she even received a degree? Did the basketball player who, after a brief pro career, went back to grammar school to learn to read obtain a college education? Was Napoleon McCollum well served—was the nation—when he was red-shirted at the Naval Academy?

It is within the educational institution that responsibility lies, not elsewhere. And it is within that all other reform must also start.

What should those reforms be? As I am not the first to say, they are three main things:

- Award financial aid on a need basis. Get rid of pay for play. To be consistent, award all undergraduate financial aid on a need basis. Money is scarce, and many need help; stretch the scarce financial aid dollars as far as they will go an equitable basis—that of a commonly used need form.

- Disband alumni or booster groups that contribute cash to students or, worse, that are separately incorporated. Do away with separate foundations that receive or disburse athletic department money or money intended for the athletic program. The Athletic Department ought to be budgeted, and subject to the same norms, controls, and financial accountability as any other department of the college or university. Until the University president has the same financial and budgetary control over the athletic department he or she does over the Physics or French department or the Law or Nursing school or the department of Physical Plant or University Library, scandal because of money will occur. We all know that when cash moves, there are tax consequences. The day will come when the IRS will have to be engaged, or when a tax-exempt status is questioned.

• Declare all freshmen ineligible to play any varsity sport. Let them play freshmen sports. But give freshmen a chance to be freshmen, that is, college students. The transition to college or university is a tremendous jolt in differing ways for all freshmen; all freshmen deserve to make the transition without the brutalizing expectations of time, effort, and travel of a varsity sport.

Informing these suggestions are two simple principles: commercial gain should have no role in the arrangements for collegiate life of undergraduates; all students should be treated the same—in admissions, academic expectations, awarding of financial aid, opportunities for housing, food, and various forms of counseling.

Why do we care? What difference does it make if some 250 to 300 institutions abuse athletics and their own stated academic missions? After all, in the vast majority of America's 2,800 or so colleges and universities, thousands and thousands of students play sports at all levels for the joy of the competition itself and to the delight and pride of a local community; there are hundreds and hundreds of fine coaches in this country who in fact care deeply for their profession—which is a teaching one—for their institutions' integrity, and for their athletes and their intellectual and moral well-being. There are high-quality athletic programs in colleges and universities that are well managed, successfully integrated into their academic communities, and scandal free. Why do we care about the big-time, or the would-be big-time? Why not simply say, Let the bandits be bandits; the vast majority will survive.

We care because all students are important—all young people are valuable—not simply our own. If all Americans ought to have the opportunity to pursue higher education, then *all*—not just most—should be given the chance to fulfill themselves as human beings.

We care because we truly believe athletics plays a valuable role in an individual's education. Athletics can be a liberal pursuit, an activity pursued in and of itself, for the sheer joy of stretching the spirit as perhaps nothing else can. There are values (and we hear so much about values in education and how they are missing) the individual learns—of cooperation, fairness, dedication, discipline—as well as lessons about limitation and how to live with failure, that are valuable and necessary to learn for life.*

---

*There are also the values taught, as I have asserted earlier, by constant institutional behavior. What values are taught by the big-time institution to that cadre of students who are exploited by the place for its own gain? What values are absorbed by all the *other* students on a campus where privilege and standards differ so widely depending on whether you are in the pay of the place and yet where the fiction is that all are "students"?

We also recognize the role an athletic event plays in the life of a community. A football or basketball game, a swimming meet, a fencing match, a volleyball, field hockey, or soccer game—each in its way brings the interested together, gathers the clan, makes of a crowd a community. And we know the sharp, keen, irreplaceable taste of victory—how the pride surges, how loyalty to one another and to the larger institution is forged in such moments, how cohesion and joy and connection each to each galvanize all of us, participant and spectator, when we win. The moment may be fleeting, but the emotion never finally fades.

All of this is why we care.

And we care not simply because individuals are important per se, or because athletics is valuable as part of education. We also care because the whole educational enterprise is connected, and it is wrong to say, Let them go; we will watch their banditry from our high place on the hill. It is important to care about the state of athletics at the collegiate level because it is indissolubly linked, in the public mind, with education at the collegiate level.

While Secretary Bennett flails away at the high cost of college, by which he means the high cost of about forty-five private institutions nationally; and while Allan Bloom and E. D. Hirsch stun and amaze themselves (as much as anyone else) with doleful laments about how American higher education provides no standards, has no sense of important moral and ethical questions, and merely caters to kids who do not know the century in which Columbus discovered America, the public at large is way ahead of the professionals when it comes to having lost faith in the schools and the means of education—primary, secondary, and collegiate. Bennett, Bloom, and Hirsch have scored their marketing successes because for almost two decades the American people have been aware of and dismayed by the gap in the nation's colleges and universities, the gap between grand, traditional, and almost wholly unexamined professions of high principle, lofty mission, and splendid purpose, and institutional behavior that is often venal, self-serving, and shoddy. The public has watched institutions of higher education, public and private, become another special-interest group, pressing for regulatory relief or federal money, unaccountable to anyone as they insist on saving the nation's soul (as they did in the late sixties) or passing the collection plate (before and since).

And chief among the causes for the lack of faith, the eroded confidence, on the part of the public has been the behavior of about 10 percent of these places with regard to big-time athletics. While not as glamorous or as gripping a reason to lose confidence as believing with Professor Bloom that there are no absolutes left; or with Professor Hirsch that the young possess no shared base of information; or with Secretary Bennett whatever the Heritage Foundation's apocalypse of the moment is—nevertheless, the reach into the public through television of big-time athletics, and the attendant awareness of how far what happened at Maryland or SMU or Tulane is from what should be going on in a college, must be acknowledged as part of the reason the public is so unhappy with higher education and so ready to believe the causes or reasons the Blooms, Hirsches, and Bennetts will provide.

The visibility of big-time athletics is immense. The visibility of the abuses and scandals, and the indifference and impotence of academic leadership, is no less visible. "If they can't run a clean, honest basketball team, how can they run a decent dorm? Or faculty? Or program of study for my child?" runs the perfectly reasonable lament. Questions of cost and accountability, assaults on tenure, the Higher Criticism of Bloom and Hirsch, all follow, to explain what something much simpler and more pervasive and institutionally promulgated has already shown: these places are not coherent; they preach, and act the opposite; they are not to be trusted. In the summer of 1987, a president's commission of the NCAA was politically pummeled in public by the athletic directors, faculty athletic representatives, and conference czars who supposedly work for the presidents. Such a spectacle did not show academic leaders possessed of guts or will or much intelligence.

So we care about athletics in colleges or universities because the selling job worked: athletic programs of a certain kind are so visible, such surrogates for their institutions, that those programs do get the public's attention. Except now the athletic programs are communicating failures of nerve and failures of principle and purpose that threaten to engulf the whole institution of higher education in ways unfair and dangerous. What was allowed to become a circus—college sports—threatens to become the means whereby the public believes the whole enterprise is a sideshow.

To reform intercollegiate athletics is to begin to approach, again, a true examination of American higher education's nature and purpose. To reform that valuable dimension of an education is to begin to remember that an educational institution teaches far, far more, and more profoundly, by how it acts than by anything anyone within it ever says. To reform the abuses of athletics would begin to earn again the public's broad-based, deeply rooted faith in collegiate education, without which neither public nor private institutions, neither the large nor the small, can survive or flourish in ways they must if they are to fulfill their basic mission, to serve America and keep her—as they themselves should be—civil, cohesive, and free.

⫸ To Make
Oneself Eternal ⫷

A liberal education is at the heart of a civil society, and at the heart of a liberal education is the act of teaching. To speak directly of how a liberal education prepares students for a civic role, we must begin with the teacher.

The teacher chooses. The teacher chooses how to structure choice. The teacher's power and responsibility lie in choosing where everyone will begin and how, from that beginning, the end will be shaped. The choice of that final form lies in the teacher's initial act. The phrase *final form* sounds more arbitrary and imposing than it should. No good teacher ever wants to control the contour of another's mind. That would not be teaching; it would be a form of terrorism. But no good teacher wants the contour of another's mind to be blurred. Somehow the line between

Delivered, in somewhat different form, as a Phi Beta Kappa lecture at Yale and circulated in revised form as the Annual Report of the President, March 1980.

encouraging a design and imposing a specific stamp must be found and clarified. That is where the teacher first begins to choose.

In selecting what will be taught, in that lifetime of selecting, the teacher decides first what is important, what skein of implications and affiliations and hints and directions waits to be woven. And in choosing where to begin, all these choices begin to be displayed, if only to the mind that hopes they will exist. Teaching is an instinctual art, mindful of potential, craving of realizations, a pausing, seamless process, where one rehearses constantly while acting, sits as a spectator at a play one directs, engages every part in order to keep the choices open and the shape alive for the student, so that the student may enter in, and begin to do what the teacher has done: make choices.

These impressions of teaching will doubtless strike many as too unspotted by reality. In this account, there is no bad weather, no child at home with strep throat. There is no unprepared teacher. There is no recognition that students, or teachers, or books can be boring or deeply garbled. I have projected a process of choice and shape as if teaching were really what the ancients and their Renaissance emulators said it was, a sculpting process, whereby the clay or stone or wax, inorganic material but malleable, could, through choices, be made to take a shape that nature never saw, a shape art supplies to the stuff the world provides. While I do not think teaching is as painless or effortless as I may have made it sound, I do believe it is essentially the ethical and aesthetic activity I propose. I do believe that it involves the making and setting of right and wrong choices in the interests of a larger, shaping process and that the deep thrill a teacher can experience comes from the combination of these activities, so that you feel what you think, do what you talk about, judge as you talk about judgment, proceed logically as you reveal logical structure, clarify as you talk about clarity, reveal as you show what nature reveals—all in the service of encouraging the student in imitation and then repetition of the process you have been summoning, all so that the student may turn himself not into you but into himself.

No human activity can proceed without making choices—critical acts of the mind—and teaching, which embraces any subject or discipline, is about how to make a choice. That is the ethical impulse in teaching—to tell how to go about acquiring the material and then building the edifice of a belief. And from the architectonics of choices a person will emerge, a person who knows how to cope with the radical loneliness we all inherit and the vast population of decisions we all live in, a person who can carry on.

If choosing is what the teacher does and wants the student to learn to do, choosing is also what binds them, teacher and student, and binds us all, each to one another. It is not the only thing, but it is an essential thing. How we choose to believe and speak and treat others, how we choose a civic role for ourselves, is the deepest purpose of a liberal education and of the act of teaching.

Teaching is an emblem of our civic life because teaching is, in every sense of the word, a deeply conventional act, that is, an act of convening, sanctioned by usage, for the purpose of making a covenant. In an agreed-upon context it brings together minds so that a second agreement may be struck and acted upon, an agreement that there is, for the sustenance of our lives, a shared principle of sharing.

Teaching is an assertion of the common capacity of the human mind to make and sustain a context in which another mind makes back, and thus makes anew. In the mutuality of minds—which does not necessarily mean agreement or acquiescence or domination—there is a recognition of mutual receptivity. And in the receptivity there is, every time, every day, everywhere, another example of the way human minds can find a common ground and clear it and build a city where people live together.

In this civic sense, teaching is a political act in that it seeks to construe a polity, defined by shared responsibility and authority. Every classroom is an act of making citizens in the realm of that room, and every room is a figure for the larger community. And the purpose of that activity—beyond the content of the class or the subject matter or discipline, regardless of at what "level" the activity occurs—is the perpetuation of how knowledge is acquired and shared and made perpetual. When in canto XV of the *Inferno* Dante meets his old teacher Brunetto Latini, he says to Brunetto, *"M'insegnavate come l'uom s'etterna";* he says, with respect and affection, "You taught me how a person makes himself eternal." Beneath the fact that Brunetto, minor poet, taught Dante, God's scribe, how writing poetry allows us to outlast time, is a deeper perception. And that is how teaching is self-perpetuation, perpetuation of the self in the students who find themselves; a perpetuation not of blood or even of similarity but a disinterested perpetuation, a giving to others the gift of how to share their desire that humankind survive as it should, with dignity and energy and moral purpose. At its best, teaching must lead us out of ourselves, into a shared understanding that our hope for a decent, civilized life depends for its very existence upon others' sharing the same hope.

I wish to speak of teaching in a civil society because I have sensed for some time how undervalued the profession of teaching has been. Here is the shadow in my subject. Teachers, in grammar or high schools, in colleges or universities, in places large and small, public and private, new or old, have never truly been cherished by this country in a way that is equal to the importance the country so clearly attaches to them. An excessive assertion? Consider some of the folk myths or popular images America clings to about teachers.

There is the vision of the one-room schoolhouse, once a reality, now a fact in only remote parts of the country. It is, however, still a benign image, burnished by nostalgia—particularly by those who have never known one—because it seems such a perfect form of the collaborative society. Then there is a more problematic figure, the mythical splendid spinster, the "schoolmarm," a version of the Minerva Armata, the single-minded, much corseted, always middle-aged female, childless and endlessly maternal, whose role in society was to take care of its children without having any of her own, a figure meant to teach man how to make himself eternal but springing full-grown herself from the Jovian brow of Normal School. That mythical figure begins to tell us that in America, teaching is "female," or at best androgynous, a necessary art whose potency must be contained. And kept peripheral.

The college teacher, who is my special focus, is in popular myth a bumbler, prey to malign influences because he is so innocent, a figure unfit for the rigors of what is still constantly called "the real world," as if schools at any level were not real, or were not part of the reality of America. At best, the popular image of the college teacher, endlessly retailed by television or popular literature, is that of a rumpled child, fit to tend his grazing herd of adolescents across academic groves but totally lost before machines, money, and worldly temptation. He is always dressed out of season, often has an accent, and is, if anything, more peripheral and weaker than the frontier woman who teaches below him in the system. If she was your maiden aunt, he is her pale brother.

Popular images are caricatures, their heightened features reflecting society's submerged convictions. Perhaps we should ignore them, but that would be to ignore ourselves, and how we think of the teacher. At bottom, these images and their variants show us figures who have either never been out there or who have retreated back in here, and who in both cases do not really do anything. They go to class but not to the office. They meet neither trains, payrolls, nor the public; what they sell cannot be seen and probably, therefore, does not exist. If it does, it is suspect.

Beyond caricature, there are other misapprehensions. There is, for instance, a widespread conviction that college and university teachers seem to require a peculiar form of job security, called tenure. Such has been the result of the academic community's remarkable lack of success in communicating the nature of its work. Academe has never persuaded the society at large that tenure is not job security only, as it can (perhaps improperly) be construed in civil services or labor unions or the partnerships of law firms, but that it is the manifestation of a principle called academic freedom, a principle that says one must have the right, responsibly, freely, to pursue and express the truth as one sees it. The principle of academic freedom is not intended to buffer incompetence in teaching from the consequences of an open, competitive marketplace of ideas. Tenure, embodying in a word a principle and a whole set of policies for its assumption, is not a perfect device for the protection of the free inquiry into the truth. But tenure is essential to the ideal of free inquiry, and that ideal is the essence of the mission of a college or university in a free society. Have we strayed from our subject? I think not. The role of the teacher is linked to the nature of the institution in which the teaching is performed, and to the nature of the society that the institution serves.

The popular view of the marginality of certain types of teachers has traditionally found its response in academic hauteur, in college and university teachers' overreacting to a sense of marginality by asserting a view of themselves as a mandarin class. This new class believed that if society would not value them, even as it sent them society's young, then they would scorn a society that entrusted its future to those it treated as servants. Academic people in America have often felt undervalued and therefore have tended to overappreciate themselves. It would have been better to assert the central value of the profession rather than to claim more for professors than anyone else, particularly they themselves, in their heart of hearts, would have been willing to grant.

In short, college teachers in this country have often been defensive and at times have allowed teaching to go undefended. And in the last twenty-five to thirty years in America certain events that have had a direct impact on how college and university teachers believe themselves viewed by the larger society have not enhanced either the academic profession's estimate of itself or the society's judgment of the profession. I refer specifically to the era of Senator Joseph McCarthy in the 1950s and to the period of the student disturbances in the mid-1960s and early 1970s. In both cases, the academic profession, in the first instance more as individuals, in the second as individuals involved in a certain activity, felt itself under assault. Regardless of the precise issues, in both periods there lingered, within colleges and universities and without, a sense of misplacement and incapacity. Whether the code word was *subversion* or *irrelevance;* whether the epithets were *egghead* or *pointy head* or Archie Bunker's *meathead;* whether the insult to the body of the academy was coming from the center of government or from the center of the campus—which is to say, from the citizenry—it was an assault on those who had chosen in some form to make with their minds, and it reminded the teacher of his supposedly marginal status.

There were those teachers and others who resented this view, which they knew to be false but which they believed to be the inevitable consequence of certain strains in the culture. There were others who embraced this view, their reason being that if such were the centers, they would gladly be eccentric; if such were the inhumane values of a senator or the SDS, they wanted none of it. But when the waving of lists and of placards passed, when the similar sloganeering of right and left had grown hoarse and was discredited, when ideological frenzy had revealed itself as a lust for personal power masquerading as the public good, what was left? A profession remained that had never relied upon politicians for approbation but that had never before suffered the opprobrium of students. A profession survived that, while never counting on society's smile from the center of political power for a sense of reward, had always counted on and now had lost the center it had always known best, the students. A profession survived but now baffled and shocked. The profession that McCarthy and the Movement said had betrayed its deepest obligations to the country and contemporary society now felt itself in the early 1970s more isolated than ever, made up of people more alone than anyone elsewhere could know. It was a profession that, in secret ways, at recesses that no one talked much about, had lost something more than the approval of the world; it had lost that without which none of us can be effective as people at all, its sense of self-respect and self-esteem, its sense of dignity. What was left behind was uncertainty, anger, at worst self-hatred.

I leave out of this account the complex matrix of causes and motives that historians and sociologists and cultural analysts can and will adduce. I give you the view of one who by circumstances of background and choice has seen the past quarter century or more of academic life close up. I describe the growth of a sensibility; no more. But I can trace the growth of a crisis of confidence in the academy, and particularly at the heart of it. I can note the gathering conviction that the act and activity of teaching, which for me includes finally research and investigation and civic effort, is not viewed by those who do it or who would do it with the degree of faith in it as a noble calling, important to the country, as they must if it is to be done as well as it must be on behalf of the country. It is one thing to know that others question your worth and the worth of the subject matter you profess; it is much more serious when because of them and other recent events you question your worth and the worth of what you do as a teacher in an area of intellectual inquiry, and begin to lose all faith.

The economic contractions now spreading deeper and deeper in every institution of higher learning in this country come, therefore, at the end of a long series of events. The gradual expansion of research monies and students and faculty and physical plant in the last twenty years is not the only backdrop against which to see the issues within the college and university teaching profession. To understand the perturbations of soul nationally in the teaching profession only against economic issues in the last two decades falsifies the picture; a truer perspective is one that sees the various patterns of economic growth and contraction within the context of a vocational crisis in the academic profession, a crisis that has been going on much longer and cuts a much deeper wound.

What does one do? In addition to understanding this crisis and constantly making its consequences the prism through which one regards the spiritual health of the liberal arts and professional educational process, there are several things one must do.

The first thing is to act on one's conviction that excellence is transmitted within colleges and universities (and all other schools) through individuals. This conviction places the quality and well-being of the faculty as the most important of all the issues facing us in education for the next difficult years. Such a conviction, when acted upon, means making every effort, extraordinary and other, at least to pay the faculty at a level commensurate with its dedication and its excellence and its dignity. It means putting the genuine needs of the people who teach at the center of the institution's concerns, for they are the heart of the place; they perform the essential activity of the place, without which no educational institution exists, and through which the quality of the place, and hence of the nation's life, is maintained and made better.

The second thing to do is never to lose sight of the special needs of the younger faculty, those in the profession already and those who are about to enter it. Swooping demographic curves, economic forecasts about inflation, government laws concerning retirement, statistics about the lack of new jobs for Ph.D.'s between 1983 and 1989, the perceptible patterns of young faculty leaving teaching for other professions or of people refusing to leave other professions to enter teaching, projections about "a lost generation of scholars," or the quality of the pool of applicants of those still choosing to go to graduate school— all such measures and indicators tell only the surface of the narrative. The deeper text tells of the longer-range problem, the ferocious frustration and feeling of futility experienced by many young people when the profession, the way of life, that they love with all their being cannot or will not return the devotion in any measure. The feeling of disproportion, the belief that one is playing as hard as possible in a game where the rules are suspended, the visceral feeling of the unfairness of it all, when all one wants is a chance to do one's job, exceeds anything felt by the younger people in my profession since the Depression. Again, the solutions can be envisaged, are difficult to implement, but necessary to find. One must never lose sight of the basic need of all institutions, and particularly educational ones, which are intended every year to welcome new students, to bring new and vital people into them; one cannot lose sight of those who will lead the teaching profession into the next century; one must find and encourage and reward the best of them, by paying them well, by appreciating their teaching, their scholarly work, their engagement in the institution's general life, by finding them time to take leave to pursue their research, by keeping the faith with them, by never forgetting.

There is also something else one can do, with the younger faculty and the older, something that assumes the economic needs of all people who teach in today's inflationary time, and knows the brutal pressures on the young and the others, and that speaks to the deepest spiritual issues of a sense of self-worth and dignity and to the calling of teaching itself. One can say again, and ask you never to forget, regardless of what you do and where you go, that those who teach have done something without which most people could not do for themselves whatever it is they do; that the act of teaching is an exemplary act, of self-fashioning on behalf of knowledge that teaches others how to fashion the self; that no teacher is due more respect or affection than he or she has earned but that the drive behind the teaching effort is a positive one. It is a drive for civic engagement that in innumerable ways, through millions of individuals, over a period of time that embraces generations, results in the transmission of the values and standards and new knowledge in all forms that a society must have if it is to be civilized.

Does that sound too grandiose? I do not believe it is, for that statement simply recognizes the central importance, regardless of context or content or subject, of those who have made the very first choice teachers make. They have chosen, every day, to make themselves vulnerable, vulnerable to those others who are the future, in order to make what is made by the mind eternal. The human race survives despite itself in many ways, but it survives because of itself when it passes on the best of its past and the best of its aspiration through the open sharing of the blood and sinew of the mind. That moment of poise, when what is known becomes accessible and must then become what is to be found, is the act of teaching, and those acts in sequence are a life, in which, once we learn how, we are all teachers and students of ourselves. Those who choose to renew constantly those moments of poise with their lives, throughout their lives, are not by that choice an elect or a race apart. They are vessels as are others. But the teachers do believe they have a gift for giving; it drives them with the same irrepressible drive that drives other to create a work of art or a market or a building. It is the instinct to give shape to what constantly needs shaping so that others may have contour and meaning to their own lives that tells the true teacher that there is nothing else to be done with one's life but teach.

I think we are in a time when those who teach are wary of what they do, wary in a new way that is the result of twenty-five years or more of uncertainty and bafflement. We are in a time when the teachers, particularly the younger ones, are increasingly and distressingly accustomed to defining themselves—and hearing themselves defined—negatively, that is, in terms of what they do not do, as well as pejoratively. I write, therefore, as someone who notes his own convictions regarding what teaching is, and why it can never be viewed as anything less than what it is, lest we allow mythology and frustration to displace a reality without which our country cannot flourish.

Part Three

THE PRIVATE
UNIVERSITY AND
THE PUBLIC
INTEREST

The Private University and the Public Interest

I intend neither to petition nor to promulgate. I have no new strategy, no new complaint for an old problem or old balm for new wounds. I am neither an adversary nor an appointee of the government. I am an unanointed, lay advocate of the private university. My institution is one of them—by no means the largest, not at all the richest, certainly not the most humble. I am devoted to it, and to places like it, large and small, ancient and modern. I now pass much of my time pondering the futures of such private educational institutions, and the savage pressures that will shape those futures—the pressures of inflation, of demographic decline, of the atrophied opportunities for younger faculty.

To that Homeric catalogue of pressures (I have named only the flagships) I wish today to add another and to explore its lineaments. It is really a simple irony, forged

First delivered at the Department of Health, Education, and Welfare, March 1979, and then to the senior class as the baccalaureate address, May 1979.

of all the pressures. In the next difficult years, those private institutions most dedicated by tradition and mandate to spurring the young to public interest will be forced to become the newest special-interest group. To persuade sources of public support to support them, for the greater good, they will have to plead even more for their private concerns. They will be driven to it by the will to survive.

And yet does one really want to see it happen? Does one really want to have places of private higher education sustain civic values and necessary basic research; teach the young, and give them a sense of the past so that they may help make the future; continue, in innumerable ways, to reflect and serve the broad interest of the public, only by behaving essentially in a less and less public-spirited way? And yet if a liberal education, and a liberalized professional education, open for the many in the service of all, is to be fostered, then it will be only if such institutions become better at applying, and applying for, special pressure.

Some will rejoice at the spectacle, for a variety of reasons, but such glee will have much more bile than buoyancy in it. It will be mean-spirited glee, and it will avail nothing. For choice is essential to a free society, and choice is reduced to mere chance when survival becomes a function of the amount of pressure one can apply to government. In a society that believes in pluralism, of institutions as well as values, it will be a significant loss when the private impulse toward the public interest will be sustained only by the constitution of special-interest forces. Any system that asks for and rewards fragmentation cries for its own dissolution.

Private universities would not have it so. They want to

be self-reliant, responsive to their traditions, responsible to the larger society. Those strands are, historically, the toughest, most resilient threads in their fabric. And the larger society, while wary of them, has always wanted such institutions to flourish, if for no other reason than that it wanted the leadership that came from them, and more recently has come to depend upon the goods that flow from research done in them. The larger society has always wanted access to private institutions, and it has access to the best of them. Their quality has become part of the national hope. America wishes to think of such private institutions as crucial, though it threatens, through its government, to treat them as if they were public instrumentalities. We should all clearly understand that nothing could be less in the public interest.

The problem is that despite what private universities desire and aside from what the nation requires, such places will have to depend increasingly for student loan and basic-research aid upon government. That is why such places will be forced to become more adept at pressuring for their principles. And as they do, what will become clear is not that they have gotten their hands dirty, or wrists slapped, or that they have entered the "system." What will be clearer and clearer to those on all sides who care is how little government understands the nature of private educational institutions.

Of course, the fault for that is not really government's. Private colleges and universities have never adequately educated government, or any number of other segments of society, in the nature of educational institutions, whether public or private, while it is the nature of government to assume that all institutions in a society ought to look like governments. In America, government is accustomed to dealing with itself, with industrial facilities, profit-making corporations, commercial enterprises, big labor, armies. Educational institutions are like none of these. They are built differently, for a different set of purposes, with different histories. They cannot write off losses; they cannot pass all costs along to the consumers; they do not have tables of organization that initiates in such mysteries would recognize as legitimate. They cannot readily shift workers from one part of the plant to another. They do not hire or fire their employees as other institutions do, because not all their employees are employed as people are everywhere else. They do not draw their talent from uniform pools in the society, nor are they meant to, nor should they. When colleges and universities are treated by others as if they were like any of these other organizations, they complain—bitterly, brilliantly—but they have a difficult time explaining. Of course, they are themselves by no means all alike, even though they look like nothing else.

In dealing with private colleges and universities (and with the rest of the not-for-profit sector), government can and does deal by analogy with other parts of our industrial society. But these analogies spring only from bureaucratic necessity, not from intimate experience, and they often do not work. Thus the reality: while private (and public) institutions of higher education become one of the most heavily regulated parts of American society, they gnaw at the hand that feeds them more and more, and more and more are they repelled by the implications of their needs. Thus their dilemma: believing they must remind the young, and the nation, of larger concerns than simply the self, they embrace contradiction and plead, scold, and threaten more and more for themselves. They become the nodes of self-interest they inveigh against. You are, of course, watching it happen at this moment, and it is neither a pretty sight nor a pleasant sensation.

The government in a democracy ought to communicate its limits. A free society must not wish to overcontrol the very process by which its young learn how valuable and irreplaceable are its freedoms—of merit competing, of choice and belief and speech. The process by which those values and others are learned is the educational process, and that process has a deep and abiding purpose, which government shares and should not wish to deter—namely, the shaping of citizens.

I say that because I believe that the formation of a basis for how we choose to believe and speak and treat others— how, in short, we choose a civic role for ourselves—is the basic purpose of an education in a democracy. The content, the data, the information, of schooling can be anything in the wide world. But the purpose of education, as opposed to information, is to lead us to some sense of citizenship, to some shared assumptions about individual freedoms and institutional needs, to some sense of the full claims of self as they are to be shared with others. For some, I may have a much too old-fashioned sense of the civic claims of education and an insufficient regard for the social claims. But I would argue that without an ethically based civic sense, nourished in an individual through education, larger social claims issue merely into programs for action with no controlling perspective about what the action is for. Action without a deeper purpose is useless; it is only activity, and that is always finally susceptible to the sweet, solipsistic allure of anarchy. Historically, education has been the best stay against such confusion, by fostering the civilizing ability to make choices and to act responsibly for others on the basis of those choices.

I think it is critical to reaffirm the civic goal of an education and the way that goal is attained through choice in the educational process. It is important to say again that through individual choices, not by slogans or shibboleths or shamanistic incantation, we become engaged in common concerns. It is important to say it now, I believe, because now powerful forces press young people and their parents and schools in a quite opposite direction: away from an education concerned at heart with ethical choice and civic effort and toward a view of schooling as immediately, intensely, insistently useful.

I am not alone in feeling everywhere a deep ache to redefine everything in terms that serve only the self rather than in terms that shape the self with a civic sense for others. Much of this mood derives from the straitened economic conditions in the country, conditions that only encourage in young people (and in their parents) the need to define at the beginning of adult lives an ultimate vocation. This grinding and pressing vocationalism is not the students' fault; they hear nothing else from parents or national leaders or any of the rest of us but of the hard times ahead and of how bleak it looks and how the dollar plunges and unemployment soars and, as the century winds down and the millennium nears, of how many promises have been broken and how the glass of all our hopes is shattered. As these students remember the battles of their older siblings in the 1960s, over telephones, in living rooms, by mail, on police blotters, in emergency rooms, they resolve not to cause that kind of family civil war or bear the scars in their genes and generation; and as places like Yale (and others) break past $10,000 a year for the privilege of working hard and competing harder, they look at a younger brother or sister who will not even dream of such a place unless indebtedness is to become as ingrained in the middle class as self-loathing is.

The vocationalism, the urge to be professional early so as to have something later, is lamentable, understandable, and manageable. There is no point in making students feel guilty about it, or in pretending that work in the world is beneath them, or in flaying today's student because he is not yesterday's, living in a van in Vermont. The vocationalism is not necessarily either wrong or foolish—*if* its pragmatism can be aimed, *if* that pragmatism can be attached to a purpose and that purpose to other people in some substantial way, and to larger purposes. The dangerous and debilitating vocationalism is the one that higher education, fearing for survival, is tempted to pander to rather than to pattern: a vocationalism that is merely self-regarding, that only narrows someone at eighteen down to anxiety about a job, that leaves him or her only with ambition but no affiliations. That vocationalism strangles the power of choice in the name of necessity and cripples the urge to a flexible civic sense when that sense ought to be gathering soundness and strength. Such a willful vocationalism, urged on the young person so early and often, lacks the capacious spirit through which one might freely educate oneself for a life of some benefit to others.

It is that vision of self, in precisely the least promising of times, that educational institutions, at whatever level, must assert again, for they, like government, ought to assert their limits. It must be said that school cannot save all souls, cannot serve all the needs of society, cannot do everything that governments and churches and families and strong traditions must also do. But, in the least promising of times, schools, especially institutions of higher education, can affirm that there is no specialization in a democracy unless there is first a broad, deep base of shared assumptions and perceptions, growing out of a carefully wrought curriculum, about where we have come from and what that pluralism of values and backgrounds and peoples had as a purpose, and how important is the unity in and through that diversity. While it may feel as if we are reinventing the wheel at a time when everyone wants to go by Concorde, it is precisely now that the values, and value, of a liberal education must be asserted again, a liberal education whose intellectual core is a required curriculum and whose purpose is the development of students who can make rational, humane, informed choices, and citizens.

In the teeth of the forces that buffet them, private universities must assert again what they are: how they embody the principle of collaborative effort, how they are built of affiliations, of courses and appointments and research efforts and values. They must communicate to others their nature, which is their connectedness within and their complex connections without. They must assert their fragility and toughness, their combination of susceptibility to every seismic quiver in the society and their insistence that they determine for themselves what quality is and how it is tested and tried and proven. Private universities cannot be diffident about their artificial, curiously hierarchical nature or their essentially intellectual and civic purpose. They must be able to persuade others that the ability to pursue the truth responsibly and freely is a precious charge and a national asset and that responsibility and freedom are not incompatible desires or goals. Universities must be able to explain how they are part of a larger vision a society must set for itself—of a mutually supportive and candidly respectful culture where pluralism is ordered so that it can be nourished and where diversity is defined as a good. Universities cannot believe, lest they lie to themselves, that they alone contain this vision, but they cannot be forced to compromise their vision, lest society lose one of its central modes for seeing.

A government's need to impose responsibility and a university's need to inquire freely must exist together in a complex, delicate, and trustful balance; government and private universities must learn about each other's needs and natures in order not to maul and manipulate each other. If quality is to be maintained for the country's good, then there must be recognition on both parts that neither part gains from forcing the other to its mold or model.

There is another form of recognition that must also occur, and that takes me back to where I began. At the outset, I asserted that survival would force private universities, particularly with regard to the government, to become a new special-interest group, and I said that need would contravene something deep in their natures. In fact, neither public government nor private institutions can exist for or sustain narrowly defined special interest. In fact, governmental and educational institutions, and the processes they stand for, are meant to serve, in different ways, the same public interest and public trust, and, in fact, both kinds of institutions choke on special pressures. We share not only an ironic relationship but a much larger problem, which is how to deal with the country's rush to define issues only in terms of constituencies rather than in terms of commonalities.

There is in America a retreat from structures of mutuality to strategies for special accommodation, and neither government nor education, neither agencies nor universities, can survive by simply spinning off special solutions or by making themselves into a special-interest group. Any institution that responds only to localized, political pressure and not to broader claims of civic principle splits its polity and fragments itself.

America is in danger of overloading its political system and, hence, in ways we have not yet fully realized, its various educational systems. It asks each to bear too much. The political system, where competing needs must be recognized and assessed, cannot function when every need presents itself as an absolute imperative and thus refuses to recognize that other claims could possibly compete. Such a spirit of absolutism renders the political system incapable of the civilizing flexibility that a democracy needs. And when that spirit of special, as opposed to public, interest enters the campuses, a different system is just as incapacitated. The educational system's instincts for equity and the educational institution's collaborative structure are threatened at their core.

A private education must be in some form directed to the public good, and nothing is gained from assuming that private universities and colleges do not want to, or cannot, fulfill that purpose. A private university meets its social obligations by giving young people of ability from the widest possible variety of backgrounds and energies and talents the opportunity to educate themselves and to be educated for the full claims of citizenship. The self-reliance of such institutions and individuals must be encouraged, not eroded. Private universities must be nourished in order that they may continue to be tributaries to the great stream of American culture and not forced to become sanctuaries from it. Rather than assuming that the private sector, including universities, is incapable of assuming a civic role, it is in everyone's interest to listen and learn from each other and to cherish the powerful pluralism, and all it implies, that is the unique instinct and strength of our country.

Private Sector, Public Control, and the Independent University

*I*n a private university, we hear constantly from well-wishers and others that the private character of a private university will be lost if we do not beware the federal government and its regulatory tentacles. The private universities and their faculties need little warning. They know that something irreplaceable is lost when they rely only on a centralized bureaucracy and its various arms for sustenance or guidance. They know that traditions of self-reliance and of self-government, in institutions as in individuals, must be safeguarded. And I assume everyone knows that federal regulation can often be disruptive, or diversionary of resources and energy, or at times blatantly intrusive into the heart of the academic enterprise.

Beginning about a century ago, with the railroads, the federal regulatory process intended to bring equity of treat-

Delivered to the senior class as the baccalaureate address, May 1980.

ment into the commercial world. Since then, the intention of regulation by the government has been to overcome obstacles set up by those intent on monopolizing the marketplace or on ignoring the legitimate claims to social goods of the citizenry at large. The intention of regulation, to promote access and equity, cannot be quarreled with. But the effects of much regulation over the last hundred years cannot be regarded with anything but skepticism by those concerned with the Republic. Intent on promoting deeply desirable ends, the regulatory system has often effectively prevented that which it was meant to ensure. The process has often become an instance of what it was intended to overcome. The regulatory solvent meant to unblock impediments to the free flow of social goods and commercial efforts has sometimes become not a solvent at all but a spreading mucilage, self-creating, self-fulfilling, and at worst self-defeating—promoting a potential but unrealized social or commercial benefit often without any discernible regard for the costs or for the potential social injury that may, from another point of view, result; often expressing benign and desirable intent with no awareness at all of the complex, grainy, recalcitrant reality that makes up daily life. The regulatory process distrusts the imagination; the result is that federal regulations represent a threat to the imaginative capacities of the American people second only to daytime television.

The authors of regulations are hard to find. Regulations are created by committees; few are willing to take responsibility for a given spool of federal piety. Legislative histories in the Congress are often unclear, offering only the broad mandate to eradicate all harm. It is usually left to some agency or department to specify the will of the people, an act carried out under the miasma generated by the hot breath of remorseless lobbyists, who have been instructed to disagree or co-opt. I have heard congressmen, who were instrumental in passing a given federal bill, debate how best to subvert its effects now that the agency charged by Congress had begun to work. The agency had begun to encroach upon constituencies dear to congressmen. I have heard top officers of a department plot how best to force Congress to take responsibility for what Congress supposedly wanted because pressure "out there" was too intense for the department to handle. Excluded from this circuit of nonresponsibility and evasion is the general citizenry in whose name all this is being done. The regulatory process, often binding lawmaker and bureaucrat in strategies of mutual incomprehension, leaves the absent citizenry cynical and dispirited. If someone tells me that this is how it works and one must take a "mature" or "pragmatic" view of it all, I can reply only that it is in fact not working in the best interests of the public, and that the public distrust of public servants, elected or appointed, has roots deeper than Watergate and many consequences no "insider" ought lightly to dismiss. The regulatory process, viscous, dense, and often dangerously intrusive, is its own worst enemy. No government, regardless of how well motivated it is, can paste up again the Garden of Eden.

It is also clear that this process is not always as mindless or closed as I have made it sound. The underlying intentions are laudable and desirable, and the defenders of the process, when confronted with the effects of their good intentions, should ask, pointedly, Where *self*-regulation is so notably lacking, in the social and commercial world, what is the government to do? Is the government to be irresponsible, feckless, uninterested, withdrawn? Regulation, after all, is the only appropriate and serious response to a situation where any form of self-regulation, self-government, self-imposed sense of responsibility, is lacking. We may object to federal regulation, but the government of the United States does promote important social goals, especially when certain segments of society have no strong interest in promoting them or when other deserving or disadvantaged segments of society lack the strength to promote them. After all, federal power and federal regulation were, and are, essential to the promotion of racial justice and the battle against discrimination in this country. Here federal regulation made, and makes, real the public interest. We may well speak of initiative and incentives and imagination and of how a free market or a free people need them, but if imagination and initiative and incentives are devoted only to private purposes, then no responsible government can sit idly by if self-interest is not and will never be coincident with the public interest.

To preach of the public interest and to serve only one's private concerns, in a way that ignores the public interest, is to ask for regulation or for revolution, and a rational people would rather conduct its struggles through the political and judicial systems than in the streets. And yet, if we want a polity less split by competing pressures, less fragmented by interest groups adept in moralistic rhetoric and absolutistic posturing, then all parts of the private sector must become less suspicious of each other and more disposed to mutual cooperation and self-governance. Self-regulation for the public good within the private sector is the only way to convince the citizenry that it need not cry, or allow, for federal regulation. In all sectors, public and private, we desperately need in this country a greater concern for the public interest, and more sensitive understanding of the civic responsibilities of power. We all need to think better of ourselves and to act on the best of our common belief.

If such is the case against federal regulation and if such is the legitimate claim for federal regulation, then the challenge to the private, independent university and college is real and insistent. It is a fact that we depend upon federal help and are subjected to sullen waves of federal control. There is no denying that the federal government is in private university education. Basic research in the physical, medical, and many of the social sciences cannot go forward without federal help. Millions of young Americans cannot go to college or university, anywhere, for whatever purpose, without federal assistance. We must recognize that, and recognize that there is no question whatsoever that we must be accountable, in ways appropriate to the work we do, for the public's money. But we must also recognize that more than accountability has been agreed to. There is no point in simply lamenting that this is so, and that a bygone day, before the Second World War, is not with us now. The government's role in financing education is a fact, and it cannot change. Nor should we assume that only evil flows from that fact—that all is lost and that our children will own only the ruins of a once noble private or independent edifice. A healthy, mutually beneficial relationship with government is within the private university's grasp.

It will not be easy to achieve such a relationship. To work toward one in the interests of the nation entails real risks, particularly if collaboration is pursued in an opportunistic fashion on either side, or is pursued by either party only for venal ends. To understand what is at risk and what must never be lost—indeed, what must be, for the nation's good, sustained—let us now turn to the private character of a private university.

The essence of that private character is in the university's independence. That independence, the most precious asset of any private university or college, is what we maintain for ourselves on behalf of America. In our independence, our self-interest as an institution serves and meets the nation's public interest. Assuming, therefore, our need to appreciate and yet responsibly resist the role of the federal government, the central question to pause on here is, In what does the independent character of a private university consist and how does that independent character contribute to America's needs?

In my view, the independent character of the private university is defined by the following features, the first of which obviously does not separate public from private universities but is common to them:

1. The institution has, and must assert, as its central mission teaching, scholarship, and the dissemination of knowledge

2. The institution has, and must retain, the right to act as a fiduciary for itself

3. The institution has, and must defend, the right to define free inquiry for the truth for itself

4. The institution has, and must maintain, the right to set standards for admission, for appointments, and for

the assessment of excellence, consistent with its human and intellectual values, for itself.

5. The institution has, and must sustain, the right to govern itself according to those traditions and values it has learned to cherish and defend and disseminate

6. The institution has, and must promote, its civic role in supporting and strengthening the country's fundamental values through constructive criticism, open debate, and freedom, within and without, from coercion of any kind.

Those are the features of the independent character of a private university. When federal intrusion (or anyone else's) threatens that independent character, that intrusion must be resisted. Because federal money brings federal control, however, and control is to be resisted because we and the country believe in and need private, independent centers of equity and excellence, money will have to come from sources other than the government. Institutions that do not have the capacity to make profits cannot subsist only on defiance, rhetoric, and the aspiration to quality. Therefore, one turns to the other part of the private sector, the corporate part, where the incentive and ability to make profit abounds. To that part of the private sector we say that if it does not support the not-for-profit part—the colleges and universities, the symphonies, the theaters, ballets, hospitals, the voluntary organizations—one of two things will happen. Either those enterprises will turn completely to the only source of funds large and accessible enough to support them in some measure, the federal government, or they will not survive. Either the not-for-profit part of the private sector will go to the government and make the best case for its contribution to the larger society, and will hope the society will listen, and then will live with the consequences of having been attended to, or the not-for-profit part of the private sector will cease to make its contributions, locally and nationally, in education, medicine, the arts, and will close up—in either case, cease as a private enterprise.

The corporate part of the private sector has a vital stake in the survival and in the vigorous health of the not-for-profit part. Speaking from the perspective of private universities, I see those universities and the corporate part of America as needing each other. They need each other not in some spirit of ideological collusion or social condescension but in order to sustain the principle that this country must have a variety of ways of solving its problems and of maintaining its basic values. A variety of institutions is necessary to further America's tradition of mutually collaborative, if differing, approaches to the public good. In linking the educational and corporate parts of the private sector, I am asserting two things: first, that each part is necessary to the health and responsible creativity of the other part; and second, that the private sector as a whole is essential to the health and imaginative energy of the nation as a whole.

Located by charter and tradition in its independent place between the corporate part of the private sector and the public realm of government, the private university also plays another role, a role essential in a pluralistic, free society. And that is the role of independent critic, critic of the private sector it inhabits, of the government it respects, of itself as an institution and as the guardian of a process. The historical exercise of that role by the private university has not always endeared it to others, nor has it rendered, nor should it ever render, the private university immune to the critical insights of others. The stimulation and criticism from the university able to exercise its independence are as often directed at the public sector, as they have been in these remarks, as at any other part of the society. The essential fact is that the capacity to be an independent, responsible voice, speaking its convictions in a fashion that does not take partisan political sides, has been very important to America and must continue to be important. When necessary, that voice should note the expansion of government control; when necessary, that voice should note the shortcomings of the academy or of other parts of the private sector. But it is always necessary, for the health of the rest of the society, that some institution in this country—and I believe it is the great, private university—sustain the reality of nongovernmental solutions to the nation's needs, and do that by continuing to send out into the country men and women who understand and wish to strengthen the deeply important traditions of independence and pluralism that have marked our country's history.

If the corporate part of America truly wants certain of its convictions set forth, in ways that ensure the integrity of nongovernmental alternatives, and the precious values of free inquiry, and of a life relatively unencumbered by federal regulation; if the corporate part of the private sector is really interested in a free market—of ideas—then it ought to act on its convictions and support the not-for-profit part of the society. The corporate part of America may donate up to 5.0 percent of its taxable income to charity and then—such is the incentive offered by the federal government—write off the donation. Now, in fact, the corporate part of America averages 0.9 percent in its giving. The time has come to say it clearly: the private universities in this country know what they are and why they are valuable, but they need support. They need support that does not require some political tilt or ideological coloration, for that would be to subvert what must be sustained, but support that believes in the competition of ideas and in the need to sustain centers of excellence that can define excellence for themselves, on behalf of the nation, without bureaucratic or political interference.

Private universities must, in the first instance, support themselves. They must have as well the support of the rest of the private sector; and if they truly act in the nation's interest and abide by the norms of the public's trust, they deserve the help of a government devoted as well to that national interest and public trust. There are, however, many forms of support in addition to financial assistance. There is also the support that stems from understanding and from recognizing common obligations. Twenty years ago the private, and public, research universities were turned into centers for federally sponsored research. Now the government seems singularly unwilling to admit what it has done or to acknowledge what massive good on behalf of the American people flowed from that act. There is no willingness or capacity to say that having engaged educational institutions on behalf of the people, for research on space, cancer, energy, and thousands of other problems, we are better for it, or that an important relationship has begun to be forged in the nation's interest, or that now mutual respect for how work is done must be shown if something larger, the nation's sense of purpose, is to remain strong. A university is built to remember; the government too often is seized by amnesia. Good faith between them is not the result, and that is what the country conspicuously lacks.

It is now a political season, and candidates and their legionnaires are thick on the ground. There is no support from them for the historic importance of independent, research institutions. Indeed, there is not yet one aspirant or former aspirant for the presidency of the United States, or any other national office, who has said *anything* about education in general. We have not yet heard anyone speak to that process of instruction in skills and values that touches every American family in some part—that single concern, education, that in every community in the land and in most American homes can inflame tension and passion and hope as few religious and political issues can. We hear no candidate recognize that with inflation and unemployment, education, its costs and its rewards, is at the heart of the domestic matter for Americans and that, indeed, education is critically affected by and critically affects all the issues that are talked about. We hear nothing about the basic process we have throughout our history defined as essential to a free citizenry, a process that has as much to do with overcoming poverty and violence and structural unemployment and a sense of national listlessness as anything else in the country.

I know there is a new Department of Education in Washington. Its creation in no way speaks to a concern for the quality of education in this country. And no politician has been so graceless as to pretend that it does. I repeat: at a time of increasing national bafflement and chagrin, I hear nothing from the politicians about making America more confident, more cohesive, more capacious, better, through making education, public or private, better. Yet America has thought long and hard on the proposition that education is essential to a free, productive, flourishing democracy. We all know that education is thought by the country to be crucial to the future of the country. And we have heard nothing of it, in any form, from the candidates. What will they say, what will the leaders of the corporate part of America say and do to sustain what is so clearly in the nation's interest? For our part, we have asserted again, as we have before, the nature, purpose, and character of a private, independent center of learning, of a university; and we assert again the need for these private institutions to pursue their own supportive, collaborative, independent path for the nation's good. What we have asserted stems from two principled convictions: that all private institutions, however defined, are needed by this country and that independent status is necessary in a free society where alternatives and excellence and equality of opportunity for all must also be at one.

⫸ The Role of the Federal Government in Higher Education ⫷

*T*he record shows that the President's message to Congress contained a request for a substantial federal initiative and that the gentleman from Maryland rose in the House to object. He said that nowhere did the Constitution authorize Congress to take such an action ("business of this kind," it says in the record). The gentleman from Connecticut supported him, noting that it was rather within the power of the States "in their separate capacity" to do this kind of thing. The gentleman from Virginia, hoping to mediate, said that if investigation showed that the Constitution did not in fact give Congress the authority, then he would favor amending the Constitution. The issue here is neither school prayer nor fiscal balance in the nation's budget. The issue is a proposal for a national university. The message was President Washington's first to Congress, on January 8, 1790, and the debate

Delivered to the Convention of the American College of Surgeons, Chicago, October 1982.

in the House occurred during the second session of the First Congress on May 3, 1791.[*]

Two hundred years later, Americans are still debating the appropriate federal role in education. And the debate is no less intense. Now, however, we are assured by the President and his supporters in Congress that there ought to be no federal role in education or at best a narrow one. We are led to believe that only very recently has the federal government been heavily involved in education and that this recent involvement is a mistake.

Those who ignore history are condemned to hearing it repeated. I intend to repeat some history and to propose some ways of learning from it. My remarks are meant to show that from the origins of the Republic, education of the people, in common schools and in colleges, has been an abiding preoccupation of the American people and has been a means for the federal government to accomplish other ends. The substantial federal involvement has almost never been a response to the call of culture or to the lure of the humane benefits of education. But the fact that the federal government's promotion of education has often disregarded local or state developments, and has been customarily motivated by utilitarian goals (economic expansion or political stability or, later, national security), neither lessens the continuous impact of federal action nor obscures patterns in that activity.

The nature and extent of the federal role, particularly

---

[*] See the account in George N. Rainsford, *Congress and Higher Education in the Nineteenth Century* (Knoxville: University of Tennessee Press, 1972), pp. 18–19. I have relied heavily on this meticulous and thoughtful book. I have also used Sidney W. Tiedt, *The Role of the Federal Government in Education* (New York: Oxford University Press, 1966).

for higher education, is, as it always has been, a proper matter for serious public debate. That debate, however, must proceed in a context informed by the circumstances of history, or it will continue to degenerate into preemptive strikes of acrimony and conventional salvos of half-truth. We have had enough of that.

The Founding Fathers' dedication to education, symbolized by the desire of the first six presidents to have Congress found a national university, sprang from their unshakable belief, variously expressed, that the improvement, cohesion, and freedom of the Republic could be fostered only by an educated citizenry. In his Farewell Address, on September 17, 1796, Washington admonished the nation, "Promote, then, as an object of primary importance, institutions for the general diffusion of knowledge. In proportion as the structure of a government gives force to public opinion, it is essential that public opinion should be enlightened." *

There was far more at issue here than high principle or the desire for a national university. Building on a century and a half of Crown and colonial grants and subventions that had founded and encouraged ten colleges before the Revolution (see Rainsford, 3–13), the Confederation Congress in 1785 passed the Land Ordinance, surveying and disposing of the public land in the Western territory. The Ordinance ordered that each township be marked by subdivisions, "the lot no. 16 of every township for the maintenance of public schools within the township." To this tremendous material assistance to education, the Congress added another charge, without the force of law but potent as a statement of principle, in Article 3 of the Northwest

* Washington cited from *Documents in American History,* ed. Henry Steele Commager (New York: Appleton-Century-Crofts, 1949), p. 173. All federal documents, unless otherwise noted, are from this source.

Ordinance of 1787: "Religion, morality and knowledge, being necessary to good government and the happiness of mankind, schools and the means of education shall forever be encouraged."

Land policy was the fundamental instrument for federal educational efforts in the nineteenth century. Or better, education was encouraged and promoted as a result of land policy. Beginning in 1802, with the Ohio Enabling Act, the Congress reserved two townships (46,080 acres) for the support of education when a territory became a state. This federal encouragement to education as a public good extended the policy of the Land Ordinance and resulted in the federal government's granting a total of 98,500,000 acres of land to the states for public schools, primarily state universities. Since 1802, forty-five of the fifty states have benefited under these acts (see Rainsford, p. 44 and passim). Across a century and a half, the federal government has made available land equivalent to the size of Paraguay for the purpose of supporting education.

Under the Ohio Enabling Act, and its successors, the kind of institution was rarely specified, save as a college or university. In 1862, however, the Morrill-Wade Act made available to the states federal land, or land scrip, the income of the sales of which was to be invested by each state in a perpetual fund "to the endowment, support and maintenance of at least one college . . . to teach . . . agriculture and the mechanic arts." This massive support was extended, with the addition of cash grants, in the Morrill-McComas Act of 1890.[*]

Direct aid to colleges, rather than support to states, oc-

---

[*] See also the discussion in Rainsford, chaps. 7–8. The Nelson Amendment of 1907 and the Bankhead-Jones Act of 1935, amended in 1952 and 1960, extended and increased the possible annual cash grants to land-grant colleges.

curred between the two Morrill Acts with the Hatch Act of 1887. This act, meant to diffuse knowledge of and promote research in agriculture in colleges and through agricultural experiment stations, represents the first direct federal aid to individual institutions for a specific set of purposes. It also required an annual accounting from the colleges. Thus, just about a century ago, the fundamental pattern for twentieth-century federal aid was set. Regulation, accountability, and the assumption of responsibility by a specific federal agency are stated in or stem from the Hatch Act.*

By the twentieth century, federal policy had evolved from disposing of federal land as a way of avoiding the constitutionally based objection against expending public money on education (Land Ordinance, 1785, to First Morrill Act, 1862) to providing cash grants to further the use of the land through agricultural development (Hatch Act, 1887, and Second Morrill Act, 1890) and making federal money directly available to colleges and universities for specific needs perceived to be in the national interest. A long history of federal support became, in short, an increasing, and increasingly fragmented, pattern of federal aid. In 1920, when the Office of Education (in the Department of the Interior) was spending only $306,629 on higher education in general, the various federal departments were spending $11,620,000.† By 1947, a generation, a depression, and

---

* Rainsford, Chap 9. After the Hatch Act and through its extensions, the Adams Act of 1906 and the Smith-Lever Act of 1914, the Department of Agriculture became the main federal source of federal aid.

† Rainsford, pp. 112, 132. Rainsford notes the transition from support to aid throughout his study.

another war later, the Bureau of the Budget noted that federal expenditures at the "post–high school level" passed through fifteen different agencies and totaled $1,772,-000,000.[*] The fragmentation and increase occurred because research had become a federal enterprise.

The first federal research contract was negotiated in 1836 with the Franklin Institute of Philadelphia; half a century later, the Hatch Act had specified areas of agricultural research (Rainsford, pp. 74, 123). The twentieth century, however, saw research vastly expand under federal sponsorship. To note the various acts of the Congress concerned with sponsoring research (the National Cancer Institute Act of 1937; the National Science Foundation Act of 1950; the National Defense Education Act of 1958) is only to hint at the full story. A recent commission of the federal government tells the story most succinctly:

> Before [World War II,] the federal government financed about 15% of the nation's research and development . . . effort, mostly in agriculture, but also in a few small health programs. The wartime crash effort in military research raised the federal share of the country's research activities to about 80%, or $3 billion. In order to utilize the nation's existing R & D resources, much of this money was channeled to the universities. . . . By 1960, the federal government was spending $750 million on research in institutions of higher education and providing two-thirds of higher education's research money. . . .

[*] Chester E. Finn, Jr., *Scholars, Dollars, and Bureaucrats* (Washington, D.C.: Brookings Institution, 1978), p. 6.

By 1970, that figure was $2.5 billion in current dollars; by 1976, $3.4 billion.*

The emphasis on military-related research declined in the late fifties; in the sixties, space-related research was dominant, while the seventies and eighties have seen the biomedical sciences take the major share. An extraordinary amount of money is spent by the federal government for specific programs of research in public and private institutions of higher education. The results have been various. Institutions have expanded, become dependent, and been improved. Regulations and accountability have become battlegrounds for those in government and for those in universities alike. Fear of federal control has spread. Enormous benefits to the nation and to the world have accrued in food production, health care, information handling, and a myriad of other areas. As usual, nothing is got for nothing.

Massive as the federal role has been in terms of supporting university-based basic research, the public monies expended on student aid have been far greater. As the government passed from general support of institutions in the mid-nineteenth century to grants and contracts for specific programs of research in the mid-twentieth century, it seems—in retrospect—inevitable that the movement toward more specific targets of support would eventually, after institutions and research programs, fasten on individual students. In the Servicemen's Readjustment Act of 1944

---

* Advisory Commission on Intergovernmental Relations Report, A-82 (Washington, D.C., May 1981), "The Evolution of a Problematic Partnership: The Feds and Higher Ed," p. 14; also p. 5, table 3. This ACIR Report and its companion on the federal government and elementary and secondary education, A-81 (Washington, D.C., March 1981), are very useful documents.

(the GI Bill), it did. Again, the war extended and dramatically reshaped previous patterns of government support for individuals. During the Depression, the government had aided individuals through the Works Progress Administration (WPA) and the National Youth Administration (NYA). These emergency measures, however, paled before the some $14.5 billion spent to assist approximately 7.8 million veterans of World War II to pursue an education. Assistance under the Act was later extended to veterans of the Korean War and, in 1966, to veterans of the Vietnam War.[*]

While the fellowship provisions of research-oriented acts in the fifties extended the principle of aiding individuals directly, it was in the surge beginning with the Economic Opportunity Act of 1964 and extending through the Higher Education Amendments of 1968 and education amendments of 1972 and 1976 that aid to students expanded dramatically. In 1960, federal student aid was $600 million (in current 1981 dollars), or about 35 percent of the total federal expenditure for education; in 1977, it was $7.3 billion, or about 62 percent of the total.[†]

The explosion of federal assistance to students in higher education was part of a larger federal policy to provide equality of opportunity and greater access to facilities through all levels of education. Since *Brown* v. *Board of Education, Topeka* (1954) and the Civil Rights Act of 1964, schools and the means of education at all levels have been one of the primary focuses of this federal policy. The deep concern with promoting equal opportunity in

[*] Tiedt, p. 24, on Depression programs; p. 25, on the GI Bill.

[†] ACIR, A-82, p. 5, table 3, and p. 8.

education is not, however, an invention of the last two decades. The intertwining of educational opportunity for all and federal policy goes back to the Morrill Act of 1862 and to the creation of the first Department of Education, in 1867.[*] Equal access to education and its benefits animated in part the vast movement, fed and resisted by European influences, throughout the nineteenth century for universal state-supported education at the grammar and high school level.[†] Again, the roots go back to the beginning—to Jefferson's hope for a native "natural aristocracy of talent" rather than a European "artificial aristocracy of birth." Such a group, he wrote John Adams on October 28, 1813, would be identified through a "free school" in each ward or township, the "best" then moving to a free education at a "district school," the "most promising" then to the university. "Worth and genius would thus have been sought out from every condition of life, and completely prepared by education for defeating the competition of wealth and birth for public trusts." [‡]

Throughout our history, we have entertained—usually simultaneously—a vast array of notions about education. It has been thought of, correctly, as a process: to instill a

---

[*] Rainsford, p. 102 ff. See also Tiedt, p. 19, and ACIR, A-81, p. 13 and notes and n. 34.

[†] Rainsford, p. 74. See also Carl F. Kaestle, "Between the Scylla of Brutal Ignorance and the Charybdis of a Literary Education: Elite Attitudes toward Mass Schooling in Early Industrial England and America," in L. Stone, ed., *Schooling and Society: Studies in the History of Education* (Baltimore: Johns Hopkins University Press, 1976), pp. 177–91.

[‡] The text is in the extremely useful compilation with commentary of Theodore Rawson Crane, *The Dimensions of American Education* (Reading, Mass.: Addison-Wesley, 1974), p. 20.

cohesive devotion to what Jefferson called "a due degree of liberty"; to fulfill individual potential of mind and spirit; to inculcate community values; to transmit culture. It has also, and less compellingly, been viewed as the royal road to social contacts, or social respectability, or social success; as necessary to a good job or a presentable marriage; as something between a right and a luxury, somewhere between voting and boating. It is often spoken of, because so conceived, as a consumer staple or a perishable but necessary appliance. Lately, we have learned to extol it as an "investment," as if it were a municipal bond or a home.

Americans believe education is good for you, young and old alike—though there is a persistent strain in American culture that believes a little goes a very long way and a lot is the result of not being able to do anything. We talk about it constantly, see it everywhere, and have developed a three-hundred-year-old habit of wrapping our political wolves in educational sheepskin. To write American educational history is in profound and varied ways to write the history of the American people.

Because our educational history cannot be separated from our national history, a sketch of a small portion such as I have attempted must be radically selective. And in that selectivity, biases are displayed, as I am sure I have displayed mine, at every turn. Yet there are some conclusions one can draw from our review of the federal involvement with higher education that are not simply in the eye of the observer. Let me suggest a few.

There has been a federal role in education in America, and it has existed from the beginning of the Republic. At times, it has been oblique or hesitant, at other times direct and forceful. While it is true that education has often been the side effect of some federal act, it is also true that rarely has it been an unintended side effect of federal policy. The federal role has been most direct in times of national emergency—war, depression, or a period of reconstruction. At our first moment of national composition, and at those later times when we needed to recompose ourselves, schools and the means of education were the glass through which the people and their national representatives most powerfully focused America's needs.

Throughout it all, in ways appropriate to the times, the federal government has managed to find ways to discharge its obligations to our common life without substantially undermining community responsibilities or infringing upon individual freedom. Now the Congress, now a President, at other times the Supreme Court, has taken the lead in releasing, or restraining, the federal energy with regard to education. For a period, public resources and monies went to states, then to institutions and individuals. Moral Soundness, Civic Cohesion, Economic Improvement, National Security—various have been the banners flown by the government during the past two centuries as it has tried simultaneously to catch the mood of the people, assess the nation's needs, justify to itself its acts, and make an acceptable political deal in order to do something either about or for education. There has no more been a consensus about the federal role in education throughout our history than there has been a uniform educational system in our country. But while the federal government has never wished to manage or control education, because the people would not have it, and while it has never believed, save spasmodically, that education was a direct federal responsibility, the federal government has also never strayed far from its posture of persistent vigilance at the flame of America's educational hopes. Because the people have always refused to cede local authority for education to the federal government but have regarded the vast crazy quilt of individual educational institutions and systems as a national asset, the federal government has often seemed baffled and annoyed by education, caught between keeping its hands off and being accused of indifference to one of American civilization's most important concerns.

The current administration is as confused, and confusing, on the subject of education as many, though not all, of its predecessors. We are now in one of those periods, after a terrible war and in the midst of economic decline and uncertain national purpose, when we must recompose ourselves, when the people and its political process must focus on renewal. We are in a period when, from the viewpoint of history, education would have been one of the means to regeneration of spirit and achievement. Yet, with productivity stagnating, unemployment (and unemployability) high, technology lagging behind that of foreign competitors, the economy palsied, and the public schools in desperate need of help, the administration has proposed to cut real budgetary authority for education in fiscal 1983 by 43 percent from 1981 and to cut another 26 percent by 1985—$10 billion in four years.[*] This is a drastic and, I believe, disproportionate cut in our nation's future quality, productivity, and strength. I think it is a fiscally shortsighted and socially perilous course.

[*] Henry J. Aaron et al., "Nondefense Programs," in *Setting National Priorities: The 1983 Budget,* ed. Joseph A. Pechman (Washington, D.C.: Brookings Institution, 1982), pp. 136–37. The analysis of the impact on education extends to p. 146.

It is not, however, the only federal course being set. The President is setting another course. While his aides speak of the need to remove the federal budgetary presence in education, or to remove much of education from the federal budget, the President is putting the suasive power of his office behind a Constitutional amendment to allow for prayer in the public schools and behind a program of tax-tuition credits. While there were, of course, earlier forms of federal subsidy to students or their families, very few were, like tax-tuition credits, awarded on grounds other than financial need or intellectual merit or service to the country. Clearly the President cares deeply about issues of social choice and personal morality, and clearly he believes that the federal government, under his leadership, has a powerful role to play in promoting those goals through the nation's schools. Whether the Congress and the people will share the President's version of the appropriate federal involvement in the schools, essentially a moral one, remains to be seen.

The Administration's proposed and actual cuts in federal support and the President's view of the schools as means to other moral ends are two courses set by the federal government for itself. The third course is that of Secretary of Education Terrel Bell, contained in his proposal of August 1981, for the conversion of the nation's second Department of Education once again to something else.* The Secretary lists among the goals of a new federal foundation for education the assistance of needy students, the advancement of equality of opportunity, the support of research, and the enhancement of state and local capacities to edu-

* For analysis and excerpts of Secretary Bell's memorandum to President Reagan of August 1981, see *Education Week,* September 7, 1981.

cate. The Secretary's proposal, no less traditional in historical terms than the other, current federal desires to save money and reform the moral environment, is in my opinion the most responsive of the three to America's needs.[*] His proposal has, however, been ignored. That is a great shame. Without attention and without some proportionate share of the public's money, the public's hopes embodied in his laudable and sensible goals will be thwarted.

The federal government must focus on education and still the Babel of bold assertions of federal noninvolvement when it is deeply involved. It must cease sending contradictory or competing messages to itself and the nation. The chaos in Washington swirling around education and all it means does not reflect the people's deep and abiding sense of the importance of that variegated, unifying, intellectual, and cultural process. No administration should underestimate the quasi-religious faith the people have in education and the extent, therefore, to which they expect the federal administration, of whichever party, to share their concern. Any administration must understand that Americans think education is too important to be construed as if it were a partisan issue.

The appropriate federal role in education is to clarify national hopes, to persuade us to move toward national goals, to bear its financial share with our money. Specifically, it is to assist needy students to obtain an education on their merit, to advance equality of opportunity in and through education, to support basic research, and to enhance local and state capacities to educate—particularly

---

[*] Subsequent developments have shown an abandonment of Bell's reasonable reforms and the strident engagement of the "moral" agenda.

through promoting excellence in our public high schools at the local level by encouraging the collaboration of school systems and local colleges and universities to work on improving high school curricula, on raising the morale of schoolteachers, and on elevating the motivation of students.

To tell the people we must renew America and then to ignore the need for a clear policy and adequate funding in education is to invite eventually the people's collective derision. The tough realities of America's future, and the historical principles on which that future must be based, demand a clear voice and responsible assistance. Schools and the means of education are among our most precious assets—too important to be left to the federal government, too important not to be fostered by our national leadership in appropriate and imaginative ways. Without an unambiguous call to excellence and equity through education, and without proportionate federal support, there can be no true renewal, for us or for our children or for our country.

⫸ *Science and the University* ⫷

*T*here are both difficulties and challenges in doing basic research in science in a research university. Basic research is not, of course, confined to the activity of scientists. Basic research—that is, investigation that seeks new knowledge and understanding rather than solutions to immediate problems—is the essential nature of research on the part of all scholars. It obviously includes but is not restricted to basic research in the biological, medical, physical, and many social sciences. In the sciences, however, there is a particular style to the enterprise. Teaching in these areas—done in laboratories, in groups or teams, through colloquia, on field trips; with undergraduate, graduate, and postdoctoral students; with assistants and associates in research—is intimately and inextricably connected to research. In science, teaching and research not only go hand in hand but are often the same hand: the pedagogical

Delivered to the Association of Yale Alumni, October 1980.

act an act of investigation, the investigatory act shared with students and associates who are also colleagues, the whole a splendid, ongoing instance of intellectual and human collaboration. Of course, scientists also work alone. Not all that is done is the result of a group effort; and not everything that is done occurs in a unified act that is both pedagogical and investigatory. But the distinctive style of scientific investigation is collaborative, and the distinctive process is such that it is impossible finally to distinguish research from teaching, seeking from sharing.

The number of dollars involved in supporting and furthering this kind of basic research is immense. They are largely federal dollars, which is to say taxpayers' dollars. In constant 1972 dollars, the government spent $2.8 billion on basic research in 1978, up $1.8 billion since 1960, when the reaction to Sputnik was in full flight. In 1958, 32 percent of all basic research in America was done in universities; by 1978, 52 percent was being done there. And in those universities, 72 percent of the money for basic research came in 1978 from the federal government. The result of this federal support to university-based science has been tremendous improvements in the life of America's citizens. In health care, in the production of food, in the handling of information—in the quality of our life—our government has brought about massive benefits by encouraging science and scientific research in universities.

The federal money that comes to universities brings with it money for the support of the administration of these complex projects; it brings reimbursements for "indirect costs." Indirect costs, or overhead, provide reimbursement for expenses that cannot be accurately assessed for each research project. They include, therefore, reimbursements for part of Yale's cost of heating, cooling, and maintaining research laboratories, as well as for part of the cost of essential supporting services like accounting and purchasing. Finally, these reimbursements bear part of the price of meeting federal requirements in certain areas: affirmative action, bio-safety, the protection of human subjects, and the like. In 1960, Yale received some $24 million in federal funds, $3 million of which was indirect-cost money; in fiscal year 1980, Yale received $68 million in federal money, $21 million of which was in indirect costs. Thus about 30 percent of the total operating budget of the university— a great deal of money, though not a particularly high percentage compared to that of others with whom we compete—comes from the government.

It was not difficult for the government in the last twenty years partially to turn universities into installations for federally sponsored basic research in space, cancer, agriculture, energy, and a thousand other areas. The scientists were delighted to have their work supported and appreciated; the university administrators were delighted to have science expand and, with the additional monies garnered, to have their institutions generally supported and made bigger. Everyone benefited. While the money was flowing, while there were ample pools of students, while energy was seemingly cheap, while facilities could be expanded or renovated, and while instrumentation and space could be acquired, all seemed well.

The welcome streams of federal money for research, however, opened the channels for a mounting wave of regulation, and there are now at least fifty-nine federal laws and regulations that govern or affect scientific research in universities, according to the editorial in the April 25,

1980, issue of *Science*. Federal regulation is not, prima facie, evil. The obligation of the government to protect those citizens who cannot protect themselves—as in all the civil rights legislation—is unquestioned. The obligation of the government to account for money it collects from its citizens, and to require accurate accounting from those to whom the money is extended on behalf of the people, is unquestioned. I raise the issue of federal regulation not at all to object to regulation in principle but to object to it as a set of processes; I object not to the need for regulation in certain circumstances, or to the obligation to regulate, but rather to how regulation often works. I am proud of a government that promotes equity in human affairs and in matters of the marketplace. I am appalled, however, by the requirements for massive amounts of paperwork, by uncoordinated or special-interest mandates that promote social goods with no awareness of the costs to other social goods, by an unwillingness or inability on the part of regulators to recognize legitimate and necessary distinctions among social entities being regulated. I believe in regulation but not in leveling all distinctions and issues. The City of God is desirable, but it does not occur when a landscape consists of evenly distributed rubble.

Because of excessive or unthinking regulation, the relationship between government and universities is seriously damaged. There is powerful resentment on all sides, and distrust. Goodwill is eroded dangerously, and a strain very old and very deep in our culture—a radical skepticism bordering on open contempt for our centers of learning with their strange, haughty ways—surfaces again. In general, federal agencies and universities find each other incomprehensible in structure, obdurate in attitude, intractable in negotiation. This recent and growing schism between government and universities is not created by science, but it deeply affects the capacity to do science.

It is time for a concrete example. I choose the one summarized across this country in the scientific research community by the designation A-21.

Two and a half years ago, when I first heard of it, I thought A-21 was a vitamin. I was wrong. A-21 refers to that circular from the Office of Management and Budget entitled "Cost Principles for Educational Institutions," published in the *Federal Register* on March 6, 1979. In it, the government proposes means to account for its money. It wishes to know if the money is used for the purpose for which it was given, and if direct and indirect monies are properly accounted for. The principle of accountability, as I have said, is not at issue. What is at issue is *how* the accountability will be accomplished. The Office of Management and Budget says in A-21 that there must be "activity" or "total workload" documentation and that faculty members on federal grants or contracts must report their workload or effort in multiple categories—research, teaching, service, administration.* These discrete categories must be reported in terms of percentages, and these percentages must add up to 100 percent. Like many others, I object—on the following grounds:

- that some individuals in the government must believe that the government fully owns a principal investigator

---

* "Each report will account for 100 percent of the activity for which the employee is compensated and which is required in fulfillment of the employee's obligations to the institution. The report will reasonably reflect the percentage of activity applicable to each sponsored agreement, each indirect cost category, and each major function of the institution." Paragraph J.6.

and that it has a right to require documentation of that person's "workload" even when that work is unconnected with federally sponsored work

• that some individuals in the government must misunderstand completely that it is impossible to segregate teaching from research from administration in doing basic research and to assign precise percentages to these false distinctions

• that such requirements to create false categories will inevitably result in reports that are wholly meaningless and may only bury, not reveal, genuine instances of improper use of federal money

These requirements, and objections, are not new. This circular, issued on September 10, 1958, by what was then the Bureau of the Budget, was revised in the summer of 1967 when the Bureau introduced new amendments to A-21 that would have required detailed segmenting and documentation of faculty effort. The intensity of the outcry against those regulations led to the formation of a task force, chaired by Cecil Goode of the Bureau of the Budget, to examine the issue. After extensive interviews involving twenty-two universities and more than 350 individuals, mostly faculty, a report, "Time or Effort Reporting by Colleges and Universities in Support of Research Grants and Contracts," was made public in February 1968. The first of its five recommendations began, "For professorial staff, drop the requirement for effort reports contained in the present [1967] Circular A-21," and the first two of its six conclusions read in toto,

1. Time or effort reports now required of faculty members are meaningless and a waste of time. They have engen-

dered an emotional reaction in the academic community that will endanger university-federal relations if relief is not provided. They foster a cynical attitude toward the requirements of government and take valuable effort away from more important activities, not the least of which is the research involved.

2. We need to go to a system that does not require documentary support of faculty time devoted to government-sponsored research. No real evidence of faculty effort is provided anyway under the present system, and there is no way to prove how much effort was in fact expended.

Those sentiments are as valid now as they were in 1968. Was the task force co-opted or stacked? Was it subverted by "emotional" academic members? No. On the bottom of the title page, we read, A Report by a Task Force Comprised of Representatives from:

Bureau of the Budget

General Accounting Office

Department of Defense

National Science Foundation

Department of Health, Education, and Welfare

Relevant officials of the government advised against the proposed regulations. As a result, circular A-21 was revised, and the objectionable requirements on "effort" reporting were dropped. Did the government forget its own study? Yes. In 1976, the Department of Health, Education, and Welfare redrafted A-21 and in general reconstituted those features whose elimination the government task force had so strongly recommended.

Subsequent negotiations on the subject of "workload" documentation between universities and the Office of Management and Budget and the Department of Health, Education, and Welfare accountants availed little. History was completely ignored, the most terrifying mistake of the mind an individual or a government can make. The Office of Management and Budget was also indifferent to recent events. A private and independent effort to satisfy the need for accountability and to salvage the decomposing relationship between government and the universities in the area of sponsored basic research resulted in the creation of the National Commission on Research. Its membership included outstanding individuals from the American Association for the Advancement of Science, major private corporations, universities, research institutes, and foundations. In February 1980, it published the first of a projected series of reports: "Accountability: Restoring the Quality of the Partnership." The title is admirably descriptive of the basic issues.

Among other recommendations, the National Commission on Research spoke directly to the issues of effort reporting. In these and other areas, it asserted the need for proper accountability and set forth rational, tough, workable grounds for sharing the responsibility as well as the funds. Many urged these recommendations on the Office of Management and Budget. Nothing came of the urging. In October 1979, A-21 went into effect. Then, in early fall of 1980, the Office of Management and Budget approved, on an experimental basis, a method of statistical sampling designed to provide accountability in a fashion much less intrusive for the scientists involved and to yield much more accurate and realistic information for the government agencies. I hope this method is designed to work. I hope that with regard to documentation of "total workload" the Office of Management and Budget does not remain forever enthralled by its own regulatory rhetoric. We will see. In the meantime, never have I seen the lash of federal regulation applied to a crucial area of the nation's intellectual life with such seeming indifference to financial and human consequences. In its issue of October 3, 1980, *Science* estimated that at Stanford University alone, these new regulations would require an increase from 3,000 to 80,000 reports annually, and $250,000 to $300,000, to put in place the new reporting system. It has been a long and deeply disheartening series of events, wasteful of energy and faith and time.

On so many other matters touching basic research, President Carter's administration demonstrated its awareness at the highest levels that basic scientific research carried out in universities is essential to the productivity and the long-term revitalization of many segments of America's economy. Indeed, the most recent statement of this recognition of the mix of teaching and research in the furtherance of science was clearly made by Vice-President Mondale in a speech at MIT on September 25, 1980. Below the highest levels, however, this spirit and vision have not prevailed. I hope the vision will prevail, because at stake is the quality of American science and, therefore, of a free, stable, productive nation.

What is needed? Aside from the issues involved in A-21 or any other specific set of regulations, we continue to need leadership capable of transcending special interests and seeing—whole—the public interest. Whether in the areas of basic research or in those of financing higher education, whether around regulations concerning safety or athletics or informed consent or waste disposal, there must be no lessening of the moral imperatives or of necessary accountability. But there must be at all levels of government, and of the university, some renewed mutual respect, some common conviction that it is in the nation's interest that government and centers of learning collaborate, and that the purpose of collaboration is the betterment of the nation's life. There must be some disposition to identify the larger issues and find reasonable solutions within a general perspective that recognizes institutional differences and common goals. Too much is at stake for all of us.

What will Yale do? We will continue to press for open discussion and for the responsibilities of the University, its responsibility to be accountable, its responsibility to protect the integrity of its faculty and the independence of its mission. We will volunteer to be part of the experiment of statistical sampling meant to show that there is a simpler yet sound approach to accountability. We will continue to work for collaboration. That is, after all, our very essence.

In restoring a partnership with the government, we will call upon alumni to help make our case; as citizens of the country, as members of the Yale family, they can assist in this task, and I will ask for help. We must also increasingly rely on members of the faculty for assistance. Through no fault of theirs, they have far too seldom been asked by universities to participate in the policy-oriented conversations with the government on matters that profoundly affect their ability to do research and to share their knowledge and discoveries with others. Not only are faculty members often expert in the areas I have identified, but there is also a deeper, more searing problem to be addressed. Unintentionally, the government and its regulations have set faculties against administrations. Had the government wished to split universities internally, it could not have found a better way than to make administrators custodians of regulations they do not necessarily accept, and make faculty members the bearers of the burden of frustrated resistance. The collegial nature of our institutions of learning is our driving ideal, a unique asset; it must not be imperiled. There are pressures enough on universities without our allowing federal regulations to sunder us.

And we will continue to encourage appropriate links between the private corporate sector and the University, in order to find alternative sources of money, and to seek new sources of intellectual stimulation, for university scientists. Collaboration is not a concept to be confined to the relationship with the federal government. Such collaboration will be far from easy. There is still, despite all the new talk of such relationships, a ballet of distrust and defensiveness between universities and the corporate world. And there are genuine risks. The dangers we have seen in the various forms of federal intrusion may not be exchanged for other kinds of intrusion from the private, corporate sector. Neither is allowable. One is not preferable to the other. The norms of University research remain and must remain those of free access to information, independent assessment of evidence, the capacity freely to publish results subject to review of peers. To those who fear that the private sector will impose requirements on the University that would violate the academic integrity and processes that lie at the heart of our place, I say I understand the concern and will not ever dismiss it. No money offered from any quarter that would require inappropriate promises or behavior will be accepted.

My experience is that the private sector tends to understand and respect the norms and values of a private university far better than the federal government does. Private corporations have, after all, their own private corporate norms too; conversations between them and universities quickly establish the lines each entity must respect and protect. Private corporations do not have the capacity to follow their money with coercive regulations unconnected with anything else. They do not forget from administration to administration, or from department to department, what they have said.

Understanding all this, however, I do not propose to see the values and integrity of the University compromised. I do intend to explore relationships, with any part of our society with whom we can appropriately and honorably collaborate, and I intend to explore such relationships in possession of our principles, mindful of the history of our federal relations, sensitive always to the fact that the university is an independent institution in our society and that it cannot serve society responsibly unless that independence is its paramount concern.

The problems I have discussed are not glamorous and brightly colored; their solutions are not simple or to be magically derived from a single source. They are gritty, grainy problems that involve hundreds of hours of work, thousands of details, millions of words, endless pieces of paper. They are deeply important problems, however, not because of the details or even the dollars but because they speak to how science is done. They speak to what the future holds for America's capacity to improve its productivity and economic vitality and to improve the quality of its citizens' lives through science and technology. The issues of collaboration, regulation, and independent integrity also pierce to the center of the whole process of apprehending and comprehending the world we live in, the worlds we are, that is the essence of science as it is of everything else we do in the university.

Science is at the core of the University's mission to foster the disciplined imagination. Whatever strikes at that core cuts at the heart of the University.

⋙ *Free Market*
and Free
Inquiry ⋘

In this century, the time lag between the creation of a new scientific concept and its general application has usually been measured in decades. Occasionally, however, the gap is compressed as a new theoretical insight moves swiftly to the stage of application and, hence, of wide, practical dissemination. We are now in the throes of such a movement in the vast field of applied research in genetic engineering.

At times of swift and intellectually exciting development, with the potential for such enormous benefits to society and financial profits to skillful entrepreneurs, it is natural that questions arise about the appropriate relationship of universities to commercial sponsors of university research and, indeed, about the very nature of the university. Because

Delivered first at the Graduate and Professional Convocation at Yale, September 1982, and then, in slightly different form, at Partners in the Research Enterprise: A National Conference, University of Pennsylvania, December 1982.

universities participate actively in many developing areas of science and technology, they have been seeking answers to these questions. Administrators and faculty have been considering the issues raised by our increasing relationships to private commercial firms. From the nature and extent of university and faculty involvement in the commercial application of our scientific and scholarly research. Today I will suggest, as a stimulus to conversation, some principles upon which such a policy can rest.

The university exists to protect and to foster an environment conducive to free inquiry, the advancement of knowledge, and the free exchange of ideas. Such an environment depends crucially upon trust and openness and upon a clear understanding of a set of principles governing scholarly inquiry. The principles are simply stated: the university and individual members of the faculty pledge themselves to the open, unimpeded, and objective pursuit of ideas; to the exchange of ideas openly and without deceit; and to the full and wide dissemination, through teaching and written publication, of the results of scholarly inquiry. The appropriate discipline on the dissemination of ideas is the critical scrutiny of responsible experts in order to assure the general public that investigation and citation in the work are accurate and complete and that conclusions are the result of rigorous and logical analysis.

As the university in its corporate body pledges to protect and foster an environment conducive to free inquiry, so also must the individual members of the faculty. As that environment and those principles engage a spirit that transcends the letter of stated principles, so each faculty member must sustain the university's commitment to free inquiry by fostering a spirit of collegiality, a sense of respect for and trusteeship of shared values of openness and intellectual freedom that the university exists to embody in the larger society. And, as the university in its administrative body must recognize that the members of the faculty, collectively and individually, are at the core of the university and that, on behalf of members of the faculty, it is essential to protect academic freedom as well as to foster traditions of faculty self-regulation and self-government, so also must each faculty member recognize that the primary and overriding obligation of every faculty member, in terms of his or her commitment of time, attention, and intellectual energy, is to the university—that is, to the students, colleagues, and general mission of the university.

These principles of free inquiry and open dissemination of ideas as well as the values of collegiality, mutual trust, and primary commitment exist to protect the environment for free inquiry. They also form the principles and assumptions underlying all that follows.

Both university-based research, concerned primarily with the advancement of fundamental knowledge, and industry-based research, concerned primarily with marketable application, should serve the general well-being of society, albeit in differing ways. Since the knowledge typically developed in university-based research is of a fundamental nature, it will often have a multitude of potentially useful applications. Because many of these eventual applications cannot be foreseen, it is particularly appropriate that such knowledge be disseminated as widely as possible so that all may use it if they will. Although private industry also pursues basic research, it does so less often, in part because it is difficult to capture an adequate financial return from such long-term, risky efforts.

Universities are marketplaces where ideas are freely available, where knowledge is pursued by way of the norms of free discussion and the free access to and exchange of information, and where the freedom to publish must obtain. In contrast to the university, the commercial enterprise is appropriately animated by the profit motive. Commercial application of new knowledge typically requires a substantial investment in applied research and development and, commonly, in the equipment required by new products or methods of production. A profit-making enterprise will undertake such an investment, and all its associated risks, only when it can reasonably expect an adequate return, a return not likely to occur if competitors are first to the marketplace. The opportunity for private profit provides the encouragement for the socially beneficial application of new technology. To realize profits from technological innovation, however, a company must strive to protect its proprietary knowledge and to prevent its exploitation by commercial competitors.

The development of theoretical concepts, born in the university, and the transformation by industry of those concepts into practical application are often complementary processes. The complementary nature of their activities, however, simply throws into relief the basic difference between universities and industries: the academic imperative to seek knowledge objectively and to share it openly and freely; and the industrial imperative to garner a profit, which creates the incentive to treat knowledge as private property.

In the light of the underlying principles of free inquiry and free market, we can now examine specific issues concerning university-industry relationships. The first is the appropriate nature of faculty involvement with profit-oriented companies, particularly with companies that seek to market new processes and products growing from university-based research. The second is the appropriate conditions of grants or contracts for basic research by existing companies to universities, especially when these conditions require some form of exclusive relationship, of license or treatment, between the university and the company as a condition to the grant. I should say here that there are likely to be ambiguous situations where reasonable people will have to wrestle with the application of policy guidelines to specific cases. It therefore makes sense for a university to have a permanent forum in which such cases can be discussed and shaped. My own belief is that such a forum should be composed largely of members of the faculty, for they are the university and must serve, with administrative officers, as the custodians of the long-term health and vitality of the enterprise. I will now discuss some of the considerations that I believe we must take into account in forming a policy.

There are potential conflicts of commitment and of interest whenever a member of the faculty is involved with extra-university entities. Let us here consider the specific issues surrounding the involvement of a member of the faculty with a company seeking to exploit university-based research.

I doubt that a faculty member can ordinarily devote the time and energy the university requires and also pursue a substantial involvement in any such outside company. Such involvement necessarily demands great concentration and commitment, particularly at the outset or if business goes badly. When a faculty member becomes substantially involved in a company, the conflict in norms governing the dissemination of knowledge becomes very difficult to reconcile. The burden of maintaining a teaching program and two separate research programs, where the results of one research program are to be widely disseminated and the results of the other may be required to be kept secret in the pursuit of commercial success, is more than even the most responsible faculty member can be expected to shoulder. Finally, such involvement risks putting one's students and research associates in ambiguous circumstances, such that the graduate or postdoctoral student would not know, when working with a professor, for whom he or she was working—the university, the professor, or the company. Of all members of the university community, the student especially ought to be working for himself or herself and ought to be guided in research and trained in skills and techniques designed to produce a first-rate scholar, not profit for a company in the private sector.

I believe that if a faculty member becomes a manager of a company pursuing commercial application of his or her university-based research or if he or she acquires, through gift or purchase, stock shares in this kind of company in such proportion to the total number of shares that he or she can have a significant effect on the decision making of that company, then there is a presumption that his or her involvement in the outside entity is substantial. In such an event, there should be a review of the relationship, the possible consequence being that the faculty member might well have to decide to leave the faculty for a limited period of time, perhaps one year, by taking an unpaid leave of absence to pursue those outside interests.

If, at the end of that time, the faculty member were to wish to retain the outside interests described above, then that person would relinquish tenure, if he or she had it, and assume "adjunct" status if the relevant department or school were to recommend such an appointment in the usual way. The alternative for such a person would be to sever all ties to the university completely. His or her return as a full-time member of the faculty at a later date would depend on the availability of a position and the use of the institution's full appointments procedure.

There are relationships of individual faculty members to commercial companies, even those using the results of university-based research, that the university has traditionally allowed and will continue to allow. In these "consulting" relationships, members of the faculty provide advice to companies but do not directly manage corporate research. "Consulting" can enhance a person's professional competence and further the university's mission. Our rule is that a faculty member may spend not more than one day in a seven-day week in such a role. Thus there is a limit on the commitment of time and energy.

Serving as a consultant to a company or, within the rule of reason, accepting payment in equities from some cash-poor, idea-rich company is less likely to create conflicts of commitment or conflicts of interest than serving in a role that has a significant effect on corporate decision making. A faculty member who has gone beyond any reasonable definition of "consulting" has reached the point where the question arises whether he or she should remain a full-time member of the faculty.

Universities frequently stipulate that faculty members wishing to engage in consulting obtain the permission of a chairman or a dean. In recent months, administrations and faculty on some campuses have been considering whether to require faculty investigators to disclose outside commitments and the identity of organizations involved in their nonuniversity, professional work. At least one major university system has adopted such a policy. A faculty committee at Yale has recommended such a policy, and it will be implemented next spring.

Such disclosure—of consulting relationships, of relationships with outside companies engaged in application of a faculty member's research, or of relationships with companies that sell to the university goods or services—is, I believe, the best stay against conflicts of interest or conflicts of commitment. Disclosure of this sort recognizes that there are gray areas where reasonable people might have differing views, and it provides the occasion for discussion. In such disclosure to the administration, there is no monitoring of colleague by colleague. Rather, a premium is put where it ought to be, on trust and openness.

The second issue for university-industry relationships concerns the appropriate principles in an agreement between an established company and the university when a company wishes to support basic research in a specific area. In discussions of such agreements, questions of exclusivity often arise, either with regard to proprietary information provided by a company as part of an arrangement for cooperative research or with regard to exclusive license to whatever the university is entitled to patent.

The university itself is the only entity that can enter into arrangements for cooperative research, and many universities take the following position with regard to exclusive licensing agreements. In general, the university would prefer to grant nonexclusive licenses, in order to make knowledge as widely available as possible. The university, however, may grant an exclusive license when it can be demonstrated clearly that a period of exclusivity is essential to bring forth the investment needed to develop an invention to the point where it is ready for the marketplace. It will sometimes be clear that society will be better served by the grant of an exclusive license in order to bring the knowledge to the public and that the benefits to society from such exclusivity are greater than the costs of any diminished competition.

I believe that each individual agreement must be negotiated on its merits. Through such negotiations, universities ought to insist on principles that seek to ensure that their patentable inventions will be fully and beneficially used and that knowledge with a potential benefit to society at large will reach the public in a timely and useful fashion.

Research grants from business firms raise other questions as well, the same ones raised by research sponsored by the federal government or by private foundations. When contemplating a prospective grant or contract with any sponsor, the university will first consider whether the intellectual equilibrium and human relationships in a department are likely to be upset if one kind of research is funded out of proportion to other kinds of research. As an indispensable condition to arrangements for cooperative research with industry, just as to those for government-sponsored research, the university will not accept restriction, inhibition, or infringement upon a member of the faculty's free inquiry or capacity orally to communicate the results of his or her research. In addition, the university will not accept any restriction of written publication, save the most minor delay to enable a sponsor to apply for a patent or license. Such a delay should not be so long as to lengthen appreciably the time normally required to bring results into print.

The opportunities for cooperative research between universities and industries are exciting and can redound to the benefit of society. These opportunities should not drive us toward arrangements for basic research that abridge our principles. Nor should the university ignore the potential availability of funds from commercial sponsors. We should negotiate appropriate arrangements, openly arrived at, that can further our mission. The constant challenge for the university is to know in clear and principled terms how to cherish learning, and its pursuit, for its own sake— and how to assist in bringing the results of free inquiry to the rest of society for the good of the public.

My remarks have focused on considerations important to universities. Our governance process involves the often lengthy debate, deliberation, and dialogue essential to the collegial atmosphere. It is a frequently frustrating process for outsiders—and insiders, for that matter—with an interest in the outcome. But one role of a university is to preserve and pass on enduring values, to make decisions within the context of fundamental principles unlikely to change much over time. The rate of change in some areas of science, biotechnology being a current example, can be extraordinarily rapid. The pressures arising from the high stakes involved can be great indeed. But when we come to cast a retrospective glance at the decade of the eighties, we will find that the universities that acted within an established set of basic principles will still be able to proffer the strengths and quality that attracted industry in the first place.

⋙ "In the Middle Distance" ⋘

We live in a world where the human race must decide, soon, how not to use the capacity to destroy itself through nuclear weapons that it has exactingly, lovingly crafted. We live in a time when, in the name of nationalist necessity, someone is killed every day. We see resources, human and natural, squandered or jealously sequestered; their consequent maldistribution gives rise to understandable yearnings and tremendous, dangerous tensions. We find in our own country an apparent incapacity to cope with the rhythms and dynamics of our freely chosen economic system. And in the sphere I primarily inhabit, the world of education, we sense that the public loses faith in education and that a sense of failure mounts. Is that eroding faith, that sense of failure, justified? Is it only another form of apocalyptic wailing to ask how we will educate better or whether we educate well at all? Or

Delivered to the senior class as the baccalaureate address, May 1982.

are there legitimate issues concerning education and our moral bearings that reasonable people must attend to?

I have apprehensions about the process of education and, because I see education as central to the country's well-being, about the well-being of our culture and its political bearings. My thoughts will have at the outset a personal cast, which I trust you will indulge, because they spring from a recent experience that forced me as never before to face up to the consequences of a failure to educate people to think humanely and historically for the benefit of others. I realized how essential to our human freedom and dignity an education rooted in reality, ideas connected to circumstances, must be. But I anticipate.

Briefly stated, this March, on a gray and windy day, I went to a place in Jerusalem called Yad Vashem. Yad Vashem is a monument to the heroes and martyrs of the Holocaust and a memorial to the six million Jews systematically murdered by the Nazis. To descend beneath the stark, concrete plaza to the underground museum is to descend into Hell at one remove. It is to go into mass moral chaos, and yet it is only a representation, in photograph, artifact, and text, of the horror of the camps and the monstrosity of the events and the minds that made them. To be immersed in our human capacity to be inhuman was for me to be flayed. I will not recount the reasons for that sense of being stripped of all customary assumptions and reactions, because I do not intend to exploit that horror or the memories of those who died. I do intend, however, to assure you that one may have, as I had, one's certainties challenged and one's faith shaken in a radical way by confronting a reality that is now part of the inheritance of the human species.

Coming up from underground, I was forced to face the consequences of ideology. I had seen close up, even if at a remove, what can result when human beings ignore circumstances, ignore, that is, our common moorings in our accumulated, common humanity. I use the word *circumstances* as Edmund Burke used it in his *Reflections on the Revolution in France* when he said, "Circumstances . . . give in reality to every political principle its distinguishing color and discriminating effect. The circumstances are what render every civil and political scheme beneficial or noxious to mankind." At Yad Vashem, one sees the logical extension of abstraction without circumstances, of System without history, of ideology—moralistic, legalistic, internally complete—in the hands of the true believer: insanity can result and people can die. When timeless dogmas are allowed to run unconnected to time, that is, to the accumulated experience and contending currents of humanity, an ideology can encourage people to murder as easily as it can encourage them to claim nobility. Not every bloodless abstraction will necessarily spill someone else's blood, but every bloodless abstraction, of Left or Right, will necessarily swell toward authoritarianism, and from the urge to control to the self-righteous justification to kill it is but a short step.

Why does any ideology tend to be authoritarian? Because any system of ideas that consciously purifies itself of previous condition or prior context—Burke's circumstances—and claims to contain all value must logically also wish to exert complete control. Any scheme for regulating life that systematically asserts it is internally and systematically complete, a law and a morality and a context of value and a machine for living unto itself, must logically will to exercise its power completely, or its claims for itself are invalid. The self-righteousness of all ideologies is a function of their self-perceived completeness; each element reflects the alleged correctness of every other. These closed systems are attractive because they are simple and are simple because they are masterly evasions of contradictory, gray, complex reality. Those who manipulate such systems are compelling because they are never in doubt. Burke is clear in warning us against what he calls "the delusive plausibility of moral politicians." It is a warning one ignores only at great risk to one's freedom.

Yad Vashem raised for me those thoughts, among others, and I raise them here, now, because I explicitly and fervently hope your education has taught you what an education must teach—to fashion principles and purposes in context and to treat ideas in reality. I hope your education has taught you to think circumstantially and thus to transcend ideology. It is when I think of how education must be the means to develop resistance to ideology, must be the process for you and your children and theirs to test values and to keep the mind open, connected and growing, that I think of the burdens public education in America bears and how it is periodically asked to bear burdens of an ideological kind. You and I and our children will see again and again the urge to use the schools for ends other than the commencement of the lifelong process of education. And the most recent version of this ideological thrust is the desire of certain "moral politicians" to pass a constitutional amendment allowing voluntary prayer in public schools.

At first glance, this may seem remote from you. But it is not.

I happen to accept the need for prayer and to believe in prayer's efficacy. I believe we Americans are a believing people, though as individuals we do not, and must not be forced to, believe in the same way, nor should we be forced to believe at all. Such are the circumstances of a pluralistic culture, of diverse peoples and religious traditions, and of the protections of the Bill of Rights. I believe it is the federal government's obligation to protect the right to worship or not to worship. I do not believe it is the government's obligation, and it should not become it, to use the Constitution to encourage in the public schools organized religious expression.

The public school is not the arena in which to teach children how to pray or what or whom to pray to. The church or synagogue or house of worship is the place for that teaching and practice. The family is the forum for that teaching and practice. A public school is not a family or a house of worship. Any American government concerned with the integrity of the family and the viability of places of worship must recognize that its obligation is to keep some things separate, like Church and State, and that it has no role sustaining particular religious values. Its role is to preserve and protect a pluralistic environment in which religious practice, in the family and church, can flourish.

We have heard the argument that in the past no child was harmed by praying in public school. That argument carries the very accent of the ideologue. It ignores reality— the circumstances of a pluralistic culture, of the protections of the Constitution, of the separation of Church and State, of the proper role of family and organized religious life— and it ignores the actual history of those children who in fact were coerced and made to feel like exiles from their fellows and their circumstances by organized school prayer. It self-righteously assumes that whatever someone finds completely agreeable on moral and legal and abstract grounds must necessarily be agreeable to everyone else also. Such an argument reveals the tendency to authoritarian control of any ideology in the assumption that if people are not all the same, they should be treated as if they were, for their own good.

Why do I bring up this issue? Certainly not because I believe that all theologies are ideologies (which they are not); not because I enjoy being told that I am a dangerous secularist (which I am not) or that I am a symbol of the decline of the West (which I could not be even if I did not hold, with Burke, to the relevance of our historical values and inheritance). I raise it because we Americans, whatever our differences, face a serious set of problems in our schools, problems that you will have to live with and try to solve, that will worsen if the schools and the means of education are used as staging areas for particular ideological goals.

When schooling takes second place to ideologically based policy-making, the very process for teaching all of us to think—to accumulate wisdom, to imbed information in values and experience—suffers, and society suffers as a consequence. I fear that the eighties will continue to witness what we see already, a politicizing of the schools for radical goals, cloaked in the rhetoric of morality and equity, in the same way the universities were politicized from the other end of the political spectrum in the sixties and early seventies. Beyond the example of the desire to amend the Constitution to allow prayer in schools, "voluntarily" or not, a larger pattern emerges, as it always does. And that is of ideologue calling out to ideologue, and opposites turning out to be twins.

My larger point is that in the choosing between ideologues of the Right and of the Left, I choose to reject both because they are finally, in their desire to control and exclude, not different. If you believe they are, if you believe that an ideologue of the Left is less authoritarian in impulses and acts than one of the Right, look again. I do not believe it.

In urging you to look beyond ideology, in urging you through education to accept a civic circumstantiality, in urging you to care for the schools and those processes of education that are among America's main defenses against authoritarian control from within and without, I offer the view of one person, one who is clearly middle-aged, middle-class, middle-of-the-road; the view of one not given to extremes but to the middle. My middle view is the view of the centrist, who would also, as Alexander Bickel* — from whom I have learned much—so eloquently put it, fix "our eyes on that middle distance, where values are provisionally held, are tested, and evolve within the legal order—derived from the morality of process, which is the morality of consent." To set one's course by such a centrist view is to leave oneself open to the charges, hurled by the completely faithful of some extreme, of being relativistic, opportunistically flexible, secular, passive, passionless, of lacking timeless principles, and of possessing characteristics and qualities even less elegant. Be of good cheer, for if the source of these charges is someone selling a System,

---

*A leading authority on the Constitution and the Supreme Court, Bickel was a professor at the Yale Law School from 1956 until his death, in 1974, at the age of forty-nine.

you can always, like me, find your bearings with Burke, specifically in his sense of the need to embrace the contingent and the circumstantial, the real world of history and competing values and complex solutions, those "opposed and conflicting interests" that produce *"temperaments"* (his italics), the tempering, cautionary, staying considerations that finally render "all the headlong exertions of arbitrary power, in the few or in the many, forever impracticable." To act according to an open and principled pragmatism, to believe in the power of process, is in fact to work for the good. I do not simply urge a long night of watching against the ideologue's delusive plausibility. I urge the positive, balanced, continuous operation of the mind and spirit that surges to do the work of civilization from the center without simplistic zealotry.

A commitment to believing in process, either of education or of law, in no way means one does not hold dear beliefs in equality, in social justice, in the reward of merit, in freedom to speak and worship and assemble. One must have convictions, but one must be willing to submit them to the testing and tumult of the middle distance. What binds us together as free women and men and as Americans is a shared faith in those processes by which we evolve and test our several beliefs and traditions. Fear like Hell the self-inflicted blindness of self-righteousness, where all perspective is foreshortened and all doubt is denied, and keep your eyes on the middle distance, where means and process live.

NOTE: The two texts from which I have derived much in composing this meditation are Edmund Burke's *Reflections on the Revolution in France* and Alexander Bickel's *The Morality of Consent* (New Haven: Yale University Press, 1975).

⤜ A Free
and Ordered
Space ⤛

Some signs of the times:

- White House aides assert there is a mandate to impose a voluntary return to traditional values.

- A clergyman is sued for malpractice.

- Pro wrestling displaces "Saturday Night Live," as satire proves insufficient to fend off reality.

- A snow-white unicorn turns out to be a goat with the horn grafted in the wrong place.

As you can see, traditional values, in this Age of their Return, are evident everywhere.

When in 1981 I wrote (rather than spoke) to you about the distrust of differentness and the meanness of spirit manifested in a movement like the Moral Majority,[*] I was

Delivered to the senior class as the baccalaureate address, May 1985.

[*] See "A Liberal Education and the New Coercion."

assured by many that we were, as a people, in the midst
of a resurgence of values and a renaissance of the "true"
America. Since then, my strong sense is that we have become
increasingly divided as a people; the mutual distrust among
racial and religious and ethnic groups has only increased.
Some say we have witnessed the licensing of personal selfishness. I believe we are further sunk into regional groups,
language groups, splinter groups, special-interest groups.
Does the search for identity have to result in society's
decomposition? Only when Madonna sings of being a "material girl" do we hear an anthem that knows no cultural
boundaries.

We have, as a people, recently chosen the simple versions
of complex problems, sought the self-centered route to
common goals, exalted the resort to direct intervention
over process and the patient workings of the rule of law.
"Go ahead, make my day" has entirely displaced "Have
a nice day." A real sadness is that the public figure who
most intrigued the public imagination during the last year
was the man who allegedly hastened to shoot four teenagers
on a New York subway. He was accorded every form of
publicity, our national medal.

I hear more and more public discourse that overstates
in order to seize by the throat rather than to elevate the
spirit. I sense a political style at all levels that assumes
the way to success is to massage resentments rather than
to confront realities. I am struck by how much public
policy takes as its starting point someone's envy of someone
else.

And yet, for all the division and resentment, the hunker-
ing down and self-serving code words, I also sense something else; I sense in the country a weariness with being
weary, an impatience with hyperbole and oversimplified

simplicities, a growing disdain for nostalgia masquerading as historical memory. I sense a desire to stop kidding ourselves that some mechanically generated, market-tested, poll-approved slogan or panacea of Left or Right is or should be sufficient to our public or private needs. I sense, perhaps only in myself, although I do not think so, a people fed up with being manipulated by the Simplifiers, by the professional patriots and injustice collectors and spielers of System and Salvation; by the diet hustlers, the Gurus of Get Rich Through Shoving, the aerobics entrepreneurs, the celebrators of fad, and the truckers and wholesalers of trend—by all those whose sole contribution to the public is to spot the next political pressure point to press, the next social weakness to exploit, the next material appetite to glut. The fact is we have been pushed and polled and pawed over about as much as anyone can stand, and we have been swung on the pendulum of fashion, out to Paradise and back to Basics, as much in the last twenty-five years as anyone wants. We have, I think, coddled all the resentments, studied all the nostalgias, burnished all the envies. We are approaching satiety with bumper stickers as guides to the meaning of life.

I now turn to you, and I urge you to seek out what binds us as a people, not to assent to what divides us; I urge you to affirm connection and not to sway to the music of fragmentation. I wish us all to assume, going in, that a civil, cohesive, and free people can maintain and enhance that state of being through the pursuit of justice, opportunity, and excellence, not through the sequestering of self-satisfaction or personal advantage or by way of the corrosive energy of envy. I urge us never to be complacent about what can be achieved for others, never to be smug in our own stations or status, never to be mired in a fictional past that never really existed or welded to some grand, overarching abstraction that never touches human beings—much as it may claim to save Humanity. Be mindful of what we share and must share, not the least of which is that each of our hopes for a full and decent life depends upon others hoping the same and all of us sustaining each other's hopes.

And what of the future? As you leave Yale, and I shortly to follow after you, what do we hope for the University's future? Yale has brought us together and will be a shared experience, regardless of where we are, that will sustain us. What must we hope that Yale remembers in order to build its future? What Yale must remember are matters of values, values of humanity and intellectual excellence and civic purpose that are simply stated but that are to me, and I hope to you, profoundly important. They are four imperatives necessary to make a future that is faithful to the best energies and achievements of the past.

First, Yale must remember its meritocratic tradition, its habit of treating individuals on their merit, from every part of the country and globe, regardless of racial or ethnic or religious origin, regardless of gender or economic or social condition, regardless of sexual or political or philosophic inclination—treating people according to an inclusive spirit rather than according to exclusive stereotypes. Yale's history has not in this century always been marked by such a meritocratic ideal; we all know there were times when individuals were excluded from Yale because of quotas, absolutely unacceptable rules of exclusivity based on race or religion. Those days are gone and must never return.

Let us affirm the better parts of our past, for they are just as real, when the poor, the members of various kinds of minority groups, the children who were first in their families ever to go to college, had the opportunity to make of themselves whatever they could by studying at Yale.

In the last twenty years or more, we have had for the College twin policies—an admissions policy of need-blind admission and a financial aid policy of fully meeting assessed need. The financial aid policy may well come under increasing pressure as college costs continue to climb and the partnership composed of a student, a family, an institution like Yale, and government assistance is threatened by one or more partners' pulling away. I hope in the longer-term future Yale will be able to sustain its role as partner and persuade the other members of the partnership to play their roles. It will be difficult but I think possible to maintain the policy of fully meeting assessed need.

I see no reason whatsoever not to maintain in perpetuity need-blind admissions, for that is not a financially based but rather a philosophically based policy. Our need-blind admissions policy affirms the heart of the meritocratic tradition of treating people according to their individual capacities and qualities and is a reminder to all of the larger necessity, completely in Yale's self-interest, of bringing the most talented to the College from everywhere so that these people may go back to their communities and their country prepared to contribute their leadership and lives. Yale must not forget, whether as a matter of policy or as an enlarging memory of its best traditions of merit, that when it is faithful to its most inclusive ideals, Yale also helps affirm one of the country's deepest dreams: that by access to the opportunity for education, we may as individuals fulfill the potential and share the privileges and sustain the responsibilities of being Americans.

The second necessity I suggest for Yale's future is that the University remember and affirm its internal linkages, its interdependent character. There will be external pressures on Yale generated by federal rule making, corporate sponsorship, unionization; there will be internal pressures to balance budgets or increase revenue, to make useful arrangements for short-term gain or shave a few points off principle. There will be many forces whose thrust will be to divide the University within, to divide faculty and administration, to divide research from teaching, to divide commitment to a funding source from commitment to the educational institution, to split professional education further away from liberal education, to split older faculty from younger. In the face of all these forces, it will be more important than ever that Yale affirm its character as a place that fosters the fluidity of passage of ideas, people, and programs, that continues to encourage joint programs, joint degrees, joint appointments—all the forms of connectedness that resist fragmentation into academic baronies or bunkers and that emphasize, as a conscious statement of this University's peculiar character, its interdependent nature. There are parts of Yale (like Yale itself) that value deep traditions of independence, but they must remember that independence in a part that forgets some obligation to the interdependence of the whole results only in that part's isolation, and isolation is not independence. It is the first step to irrelevance.

The internal character of Yale leads us to my third imperative for Yale's future, and that is constant attention to its external shape or, more precisely, to its integrity or lawful independence as an institution in American culture. By now we have gained some sense of the pressures pressing upon Yale, and universities in general, and some sense of the dangers of independence carried to isolation. Mindful of these forces, let me prophesy that it will be necessary to affirm constantly in the future the proper role and shape of a private institution of higher education—an institution that on the one hand will be committed to being a tributary to society, not a sanctuary from it, but that on the other hand will be more and more obliged to affirm its nature as a center for the free and open exchange of ideas, of independent thought, of minority opinion and dissent, of criticism of the culture as well as sustenance of the values it shares with the country at our best.

To define the line between assuming authority and responsibility for its own acts and acting in a responsive and responsible fashion to a sponsor, particular group, or government will require constant care and thought. Whether the issue is binding arbitration to settle the conditions of a first contract or financial aid and draft registration or singing the Solidarity anthem for the USIA or licensing the commercial uses of University-based research or the relation of Yale and New Haven and their respective resources or pursuing federal money outside peer review through legislative line items or any of the future variants of those issues, the first obligation is to be mindful—amid all the competing claims and the cries for convenience that masquerade as high principle—of what the essential lawful independence of the institution requires, a legitimate independence entailing self-government necessary to foster an environment hospitable over generations to the highest-quality teaching, learning, and research.

The shape of a university will change, as will what the culture expects or requires of the university. What must abide is the internal conviction that a private institution can make significant contributions only if it first has and is willing to articulate the special nature, obligations, and privileges of its independent status. If it cannot do that, it will lose its unique shape under the pummeling of competing demands. If it ignores or somehow immunizes itself against those demands, it may keep its integrity but in a void, disconnected. To be faithful to one's design and yet affiliated with society's needs is to approach a vision of the university's lawful independence; it will continue to be in the future an obligation to define and defend the institution by one's daily acts as well as by one's formal expressions.

These three elements I hope we will share and cherish for Yale's future—what I have called its meritocratic tradition, its internally interdependent character, and its need constantly to define its lawful independence—engage values and qualities specific to Yale but could be relevant for other distinguished universities as well. The final point I make for Yale's future is, for me, particularly apt for Yale; it concerns the need to remember that at the heart of Yale College is the idea of a liberal education. I do not mean to imply that Yale alone keeps alive in its undergraduate college this idea or that others are not equally committed to the principles of such an education. Not at all. Rather, I mean that since the early nineteenth century, the Yale

College faculty and Yale College graduates have been specially committed to a view of undergraduate education that, whatever the fashions of the day or the changes from generation to generation, holds that an undergraduate education is to be pursued for the love of learning for its own sake.

Yale's liberal education is an education meant to increase in young people a sense of the joy that learning for the sake of learning brings, learning whose goal is not professional mastery or technical capacity or commercial advantage but the commencement of a lifelong pleasure in the human exercise of our minds, our most human part. It is an education whose spirit is designed to remind us that education is lifelong and will be the means, far more than a job or career, to forge those links with family, neighbor, community, and country that will allow each to sustain the other. It is also an education in the development of that most practical of human activities, which is thinking—analytically, creatively, humanely—and in expressing the results of that thinking, in speech and in writing, with clarity, logic, and grace. In the fundamental acts of thinking and expressing, the fundamental human parts of ourselves are initially shaped and then shared, and that shaping and sharing starts in what we call a liberal education, an education in the making of those orders whence freedom derives and by which it is defended.

The historically rooted, value-laden imperatives I wish us to see in Yale's future have in common inclusive ideals made real so that order and freedom may exist in mutual play of support. And for all the angry divisions and the divisiveness that I catalogued at the outset, the vision of a civil order where we are free to pursue our destinies while sustaining the rights of others to pursue the same goals informs my view that the University must be a free and ordered space, for those who live there and for the country at large, a source and symbol of what we can be and can do at our best. I trust we all share that vision as our common hope for our common future.

CODA

⇛ "Give Time to Time" ⇚

I

Doubtless through the spring and summer you experienced some doubts. Any rational person would. In the bower of anyone contemplating the fact of beginning college, there must be some creeping tendril of anxiety, some late summer's night when the inner ear heard the inner voice ask, What is the point to it all? And will anyone tell me or am I expected to know?

You are not supposed to know, but you are expected to wish to know. And I am expected to tell you. Indeed, in examining the purpose of what you now begin, you begin to do what you are here to do; you begin to examine assumptions, hone your powers of analysis, expand your

Part I was delivered as the freshman address, September 1980. Part II was delivered to the same class as the baccalaureate address, May 1984.

capacities for synthesis. You begin to grow out of yourselves and into us, whoever us is. In the words of a famous report on education of the Yale College faculty in 1828, you are here to be thrown upon the resources of your own mind. And that means defining and refining those resources by drawing upon the resources of the place and of the other people in the place. To what end? So that the individual mind and spirit, made civil and capacious and curious, can foster the good and the knowledge it wishes for itself on behalf of others. The ultimate goal is to make the one, through fulfillment of the self, part of the many.

You have come to a great, ancient University and to the College within it in an even older New England city on the water. You are not the first, nor will you be the last, to come with your questions. The questions that you ask yourself and will ask of Yale, and that the times will ask you, are natural and appropriate. No one ought to approach an education or a university in a spirit that is settled or unquestioning or smug or certain of answers or results. Intellectual curiosity, a hunger for contact with the wider world as it is aggregated here, a desire to test one's best with others, all of that is the very spirit Yale would encourage in you if Yale did not find it in you. You are in the right place.

You have also come not only to a great, ancient university but to a place marked with its origins as a Puritan village. If you come here, therefore, questioning your election, that too is still in the spirit of the place. You will know you are truly of Yale as well as at it when you hear yourself indulging in that oldest Puritan pastime—talking about

how hard you work. One of the deepest pleasures of this
place is to spend leisure time expostulating about work.
Futile as it may be to resist a deep institutional tide that
began to flow hereabouts in October 1701, I will assert
in passing that pleasure can derive as much from contemplation as from activity, as much from thinking about
what you are doing as from being busy at it.

I raise the questions of your natural anxieties and the
need for some larger sense of purpose, of the puritan origins
of this place, and of America, and of the inevitable call
to busyness and frantic activity those origins imply, because
such concerns are part of a much larger set of concerns
in our country today—concerns about pace, anxiety about
purpose, questions of capacity and coherence. I speak to
these anxieties because you will have to learn to manage
them, here and later, and because I can better say what
our purpose is if that purpose, at Yale, is in perspective.

The 1980s are here and, that fictional boundary now
crossed, the pace of anxiety quickens. In the West, we
have a particular accounting system whereby we measure
and make manageable duration. We create what we call
time, among other ways, in multiples of ten—decades, centuries, millennia. These deep, and deeply important, fictions
represent boundaries we set ourselves. When we cross them,
we revive our sense of advancement. All cultures set a
starting date for the present era, a point of origin, a year
one. In the movement away from that point of beginning
across more and more boundaries, there is a paradox:
whatever moment is newest is also oldest, for today is
older than all the yesterdays; whatever moment is oldest

is youngest, for whatever was a thousand years ago is also, in retrospect, younger. Priority always belongs to the "primitive"; modernity is what is most aged. We must recognize, therefore, that advancement also means accumulation—of fatigue and failure as much as innovation and "progress."

When we give ourselves these fresh starts every ten years, or every hundred years, or even, once before, every thousand years, we are giving ourselves the necessary illusion that we have breasted a tape and won a race, even though the marathon continues as it always has, regardless of the little stops for breath we allow ourselves to make. The long run is made bearable only by all the short runs. Now, at the outset of the 1980s, we are beginning another short run.

Across a century, however, these sprints of a decade tire the race. The accumulated heaviness wears as we all look back at the last hundred years. The consciousness of this accumulation and the sense of decline it engenders led, at the end of the last century, to the coining of the phrase *fin de siècle*, the phrase implying decadence, that is, lack of vitality and softness of effort in the face of demands of the world. That accumulated fear of decline and hunger for hope is strong at the end of centuries and strongest at the end of ten centuries, or a millennium. Then we hear most clearly the accent of the Apocalypse.

That accent derives from many sources, but one of the most piercing expressions of mingled promise and terror is in the final book of the Bible, the Revelation given to Saint John on the Isle of Patmos. In the twentieth chapter we hear that an angel comes down and binds the serpent for a thousand years, and in those thousand years Christ reigns with those who believed in Him. But when that millennium expires, Satan is loosed out of his prison for a little season, and that season is one of war, deception, and fire, until the second time, when God opens His book, the book of life, says John, and all are judged by that book according to their works, and whosoever is not found written there is cast into a lake of fire. And that, says John, is the second and final death.

This terrifying and exhilarating vision, so important to the culture of seventeenth-century England that shaped America in its origins, leaves its mark. It leaves its mark in the details of the Apocalypse, still the details of any version of the end anyone holds down deep. It leaves its mark in the larger prophecy that complete closure comes, and that it will come in terms of a thousand years and bring seasons of hope and disaster until some are saved and some are not. Given this hectic and indelible vision, it is small wonder that perhaps 980 years ago, more or less, masses of people in Europe thought the world was going to end; small wonder that the third term of ten—a millennium—reinforces our sense of the reality of the first term of ten—a decade; small wonder, alas, that the coercive rhetoric of the Apocalypse never seems to lose its allure and that parts of us—whatever our beliefs—respond to the trumpet of Armageddon despite the voice of reason.

All this is preamble to where we think we are, beginning a new decade, beginning the end of a century, ending the second millennium. Humankind becomes more consciously retrospective the more it fears the seemingly uncontrollable accumulation of the past, and so it is with us. Throughout the Western world, the decline of the West is feared, and that fear feeds itself. In America, self-consciousness is acute, and keen is our sense of anxiety about our advancing accumulation of responsibility and failed effort. We hear on all sides that we are weak; that knowledge is exploding unmanageably; that the pace of uncontrollable events is exacerbated by instantaneous communication; that technology is a beast biting its own tail; that ideology is insufficient to an exploding reality; that the family is in decline; that traditional values are devalued; that standards, for work and play and quality of life, are gone.

I believe the new wisdom of a century's end is really only fatigue masquerading as philosophy. I urge you to beware the captivation of these easy, thoughtless profundities. These banalities have in common only the belief that we are not able to give definition—shape and contour—to what is around us. These shibboleths finally tell more about those who utter them than about reality. They are expressions of exhaustion more often than they are forms of explanation. They tell us that when the pressure of accounting for everything within living memory becomes overwhelming, the desire to control is matched, and often mastered, by a profound sense of a loss of control.

At such moments, what power consists of and who will have it become pressing questions. They become more pressing because autonomy and the capacity to define the contour of events, to seize Fortune by the forelock, are threatened. The inevitable reaction to powerlessness, including knowing what power is and what it is for, is to react the way we see so many in this country reacting: it is to retreat into self-interest, to hunker down, to isolate the society, to make all public concerns matters of private prerogative, so that the hunched individual can find compensation for his sense of thwarted autonomy in the public realm. In our country, we see a deeply dangerous turning away from public obligations that is the result of a dangerous turning inward to find sufficiency where it finally is not—only in the self. We are urged to isolate ourselves as a nation, to erect walls of tariff or trade or arms, to question all strategies for collaboration and alliance, and to embrace only tactics of self-satisfying accommodation. We are urged to solve moral problems by decree and to grow weary of processes of the law. Such are the counsels of the tired short run.

Ethnic groups divide and collide; religious communities seize fads as if they were faiths; political processes undergo changes in institutional shape only teasingly and superficially signaled by the cynicism of a free electorate. Within these cultural and religious and political contexts, we are assured by those with the obligation to lead that nothing has worked as promised, and promises have no ability to work. Promises are made or viewed not as enduring institutions but only as expedient impulses. All of what is said in this Apocalyptic Style rushes us past the processes of public reason to the self-lacerating counsels of private despair. And this rush to unreason is nowhere clearer than in our public speech, the speech our society uses for itself, the speech public leaders, of whatever kind, use to set a national mood or establish a sense of purpose. You can tell a great deal about a people's stability and confidence from the way it talks to and about itself in public. In this country now, seized by the Apocalyptic Style, everything is overstated because overstatement is meant to redeem our feeling of being overwhelmed. Whether the rhetoric is for or against nuclear power, or for or against registration for the draft, or for or against a religious or political party, the rhetoric is often coercive, pandering to fear rather than appealing to reason, summoning the specter of the end of the world rather than pausing to examine the world, within and without, as it must be lived in.

America is a religious nation without a coherent creed, a believing people hungering for a faith to which to give its assent. So much of what passes for moral certitude today covers a void but does not fill it. The void remains. But that is not yet the Apocalypse. Divisions and problems there are. But Armageddon is not yet. The race has a long, long way to go. What seems exhausted to many is not; it is they who are tired. The frenzy that sees the End at every moment sees an illusion. My message is simple: so much of what you will hear, during your time here and later, springs from a fatigue and failure of nerve that would ensnare you and your strength in its weakness. Beware it; do not be charmed by it. Do not become one of those who have only the courage of other people's convictions. Be one of those who believe in what Shakespeare called the pauser, reason. Be one for whom coercion, of any kind, whether coercion based on race or sex or religious or political belief, is an anathema. Leave the Apocalyptic Style to those who cannot, or do not want to, do the deeply human work of finding their own voices in the common chorus.

New decade; end of a century; millennium; the fact is, nothing is old or tired or declining for you. You are new. You do not need only the worn intellectual cloaks of others; you must weave your own, with which to walk out in the world. That is why you are here, to grow in intellectual capacity, human sensitivity, spiritual depth, through the process—begun here, lifelong in duration—of a liberal education. A liberal education is not an education for the impractical; it is the intensely practical act of self-fashioning that occurs as you develop your intellectual and human powers across a variety of areas of intellectual inquiry and methods and values. The purpose of this self-fashioning is not to get a job; it is to develop yourself, so that whatever you do later will not be done from a narrow or parochial human base. The larger purpose of this self-fashioning is to learn how to turn the self out, to reach into yourself so as to reach beyond yourself—out to others, in order to make a country, and the lives of your fellow citizens, better.

A liberal education is a process of self-knowledge for the purpose of shared civility. It should foster a skepticism of the Apocalyptic or Coercive Style, a tolerance for other beliefs and peoples, a passion for excellence and equity, a respect for the dignity of the individual. Such an education begins in Yale College but should not end here; it is not a product, freeze-dried and wrapped in a plastic bag, that you "get" by attendance in class or grades or by acts of faculty and trustees; it has nothing to do with credentials or accreditation or profession. A liberal education is a process, whereby we each make ourselves part of a commonality that respects the majesty and integrity of the individual talent. To engage the process you have only to embrace the proposition that by testing yourself against the new you will be made, by yourself, renewed.

I welcome you to the manifold pleasures of the spirit of renaissance.

II

When last I addressed you, in September of 1980, I talked about how we were all at the outset of a decade, one of the fictional boundaries we create for ourselves, a short run like the longer runs of a century or a millennium. I suggested that we make for ourselves these constructs of time, so as to render duration or flux manageable and thereby to give ourselves the illusion of "progress" or at least of orderly progression. And I urged you to think of how fatigue accumulates the more of these fictional boundaries we cross, so that at the end of centuries or millennia Western culture looks back with awe at the responsibilities and failed promises to itself it has accumulated. Late in the day of a century or a millennium, the culture always feels itself in decline, now bowed down by a past it has fashioned in order to make flux tractable.

Four years ago, I said I hoped you would not succumb to the sense of enervation and anxiety that, if history were a guide, would continue to afflict us as this decade approached the last decade of the century and this last century of the second millennium approached its end. I asked you to resist the call to give in and give up that is so clearly the mark of the Apocalyptic Style.

I raise these matters again because they have remained in my mind and because I wish to return today to another view of my persisting concern. Plainly put, I am concerned that people feel a growing sense of crisis in public and personal matters and believe there is a diminishing amount of time. I am concerned that, confronted by problems, many of us have no faith in time or believe we have no time to let faith grow. I am concerned that we have given up on history.

A sense of history is more than an instinct to look back for lessons; it is an habitual act of the mind to re-member—that is, reassemble—the corpus of lost experience in order to find cause, motive, or pattern, or the absence of them, so that one may live a rational, not a purposeless, existence. Without such an act of reconstitution of what has shaped us but which we have not lived through, there can be no complementary act of making the future. Without an act of the mind to create a history, there are no grounds for the necessary act of the will that alone can make a future.

I believe that what make us human are the acts and the activity of making with the mind—the affirmative assertions of our intellective and imaginative parts. The process of imposing design on the seemingly endless continuums of physical or human nature is the activity each of us engages every moment of our lives in order to be human. To understand our roles as creators of time and our obligation to live in and through what we have designed for ourselves is a constant necessity if we are to fulfill ourselves as individuals, as a people.

I suggest that making time out of sheer flux is an act of the mind; to live fruitful and civilized lives in time is an act of the will. To give up on the mind or the will, and to say, It is no use, I cannot make sense of it; I am too pressed; the human race is too threatened; annihilation is imminent, through nuclear war or the uncontrollable aggression of irrationalism, and then to say, *Therefore,* I am licensed to let go, to give in, to ignore what we have made or what I might make; *therefore,* I can give in to irrationalism, on a global scale, or as a person can be expected only to pursue narcissism or hedonism; *therefore,* I can or I must become indifferent to choice and conse- quence, to civility, to the ancient imperatives of sacrifice for the greater good, to the call of goals and ideals beyond myself—to say all of this at any level is to let go of time, that is, to cast off life.

When in 1980 I urged you to remember that we make up time and urged you not to allow the past we fashion to overwhelm us, I took as my text the last book of the Christian Bible, the Revelation given to Saint John on the Isle of Patmos. From the hectic and searing imagery of war, deceit, and fire in that text, the West derives the indispensable imagery for the Apocalypse, imagery that must always warn us but must never enthrall us. Today, I am led to my thoughts on the need to live in time so as to affirm our lives by another text, a briefer one, really an aphorism: the words of Rabbi Tarphon, who, in the second century of the common era, says in the *Pirke Abot,* "You are not required to complete the work, but neither are you free to desist from it." Recently, Harold Bloom has glossed these powerful words as follows: "The work cannot be completed in time, yet we must work as if there will be time enough to complete it, 'to give time to time,' as in the Sephardic proverb. . . ."[*]

Recorded in times of threat and danger as severe as any faced yet by the Jews, the words of Tarphon affirm the will: the individual will not to desist from the work of living a moral life, the communal will to abide in the knowledge that life is a gift from God, a gift in time of

[*] Olivier Revault D'Allonnes, *Musical Variations on Jewish Thought,* trans. Judith L. Greenberg, introduction by Harold Bloom (New York: Braziller, 1984), pp. 26–27.

time. His words affirm that to deny the gift in time is to deny the sacred gift of life. Whatever the horror behind, whatever the threat to come, Tarphon enjoins us to remember our responsibility, which is also our joy, to treat what is finite and hedged about by pain and loss as if it were infinite and ever growing in goodness, both the good things of the world and the moral purposes that keep us free and together.

In Tarphon's words, there is a tough, pragmatic recognition of our human limits, for we will never do or know the good as much as we need, as much as we wish. We will never make ourselves or our families or our communities or our life perfect. We will never fully overcome our flaws, despite our best hopes and our best efforts. Our destiny will never be to see evil and want and pain banished from our lives or from the lives of our parents and children. But Tarphon, knowing all this and more, also says that because imperfection and decay will be our lot, we cannot and must not act as if loss were our only condition; as if there were nothing to gain as well; as if we did not also have a way of finding a glorious freedom within, not despite, our confines. There exist for us all those ideals that give meaning to our sacrifices, those beacons shining beyond time that beckon and guide our lives in time—if only we have the courage to exercise our freedom to remain free.

For all the knowledge that we will never succeed in the work of our lives, we must continue to choose to continue. For all the frustrations and fears each of us has and will have in our short time, that will shatter us within and separate us each from each, we must choose to pursue to the end of choosing the best we know for ourselves and for each other, and in that choosing, long and late, we will connect with each other.

Rabbi Tarphon would have us know that our best hopes will not be realized; he would nevertheless, and this is perhaps our glory, have us affirm that it is in our hands to make our time mean something. Out of the dark knowledge that nothing will last or be completed, we can, if we will, give meaning to our past and thus make of our portion of flux a future alive with dignity and purpose. To throw up one's hands because all is not, and never will be, perfect, or because there may be a moment of such intense light that all is darkness ever after, is to let time career back into flux. It is to deny—by the abdication of the mind and will—life, the time here together.

The wisdom, hard bitten, hard won, life affirming, of the great Rabbi, and of those he followed and those who followed him, is the wisdom of the individual will that forms us as much as does the wisdom of collective fate from the Book of Revelation. Our heritage, and the heritage of those who founded our country and this University, is compounded of the primacy of the individual will and the need for collective responsibility that derives from the Rabbis and the Saints. The Puritan culture that shaped this country embodied the tension between the drive toward inner perfection and outer completion and the awareness of human limitation and the need to begin again and again to gain a purchase on goodness.

The rage to perfection and the bone knowledge of human fallibility pull against each other in each of us as Americans, within us as a people. When we are confident, this tension fructifies and charges us as a people with a strange and wonderful coherence, a consensus or common conviction that we can do for ourselves and for others more than has hitherto ever been done or thought possible. Then our will is cohesive. And when we are fatigued, or believe we should be, when we are frustrated because we are shackled, not redeemed, by our best efforts, and are impatient with our best hopes, the tension between perfectibility and fallibility breaks us apart, sends us thrashing, and we share only a desire to lie low. Then we grow impatient not with idealism, our best product, but with the absence of quick results and fast fixes, our besetting sin. Then, as now, we displace a sense of aspiration with a demand for entitlement; we substitute for an older generosity a mean-spiritedness, and for a formative principle that we came to this land to be inclusive an equally old and darker impulse to deny differentness and to exclude, even among ourselves.

This crankiness, this fatigue with wearing our best hopes on our sleeves, this collective shrugging off of the burden of our best promises to ourselves, is not the result of any inevitable historical process. It is not in the cards or in the stars that Americans as individuals or as a people need to grow soft or tired or uncompetitive or sour on their best dreams. We must remind ourselves and each other of the beacons we have set ourselves, our systems of law, our commitment to equality of opportunity and excellence of performance, our principle of judging each other on native talent, our values of individual initiative, love of country in generous spirit, helping others less fortunate. Those are the beacons that guide the act of making a future.

You are the future. In the year 2000, your generation will be leading this country. You must be the ones to give time to time. You must know that idealism is not paralyzing but liberating and that to strive for principles, even if the journey is never completed, is to tap a vast source of energy, the energy to commit to do your best in the precious, brief time each of us is blessed to have. You must not waver. I know you will not.

1137